The Art
of the Possible

The Art
of the Possible

The Path from Perfectionism
to Balance and Freedom

ALEXANDRA STODDARD

William Morrow and Company, Inc.
New York

It is the policy of William Morrow and Company, Inc., and its imprints and affiliates, recognizing the importance of preserving what has been written, to print the books we publish on acid-free paper, and we exert our best efforts to that end.

Permissions appear on page 252 and constitute a continuation of the copyright page.

Library of Congress Cataloging-in-Publication data

Stoddard, Alexandra
The art of the possible: the path from perfectionism
to balance and freedom / Alexandra Stoddard.
p. cm.
ISBN 0-688-14335-0
1. Self-actualization (Psychology)
2. Perfectionism (Personality trait) 3. Excellence. I. Title.
BF637.S4S826 1995
155.2'32—dc20
95-16639
CIP

Printed in the United States of America

5 6 7 8 9 10

BOOK DESIGN BY MARYSARAH QUINN AND MARK GAROFALO

In memory of
my brother
ROBERT POWELL JOHNS, JR.

1945

Thank you for loving me
for fifty-three years.
Please continue to
watch over me.

Love, love,
Sandie

Contents

A Letter to My Readers

Dear Readers,

Whenever I'd meet you on book tours you told me, "I need this book badly, Alexandra." So many times I'd hear stories of how you're trying to overcome perfectionist traits.

Each of us is trying to find greater meaning in our life. We find the path of perfection doesn't bring us freedom. Focusing on everything that is possible, however, is the way to seek and find joy, love, and happiness.

Many of you ask what was my favorite book to write. The book I'm writing is always the most fun. *The Art of the Possible* is no exception. We all are struggling to do a good job with our lives. I've met so many of you, and I know your character and values.

What each of us has to learn is to readjust our expectations to a more healthy, comfortable balance. The world not only won't break or melt down if we accumulatively feel more ease, more pleasure in all we do; together, we will be making a big difference in our society.

By making minor shifts in our attitudes and our willful standards, we will find everything eventually works itself out, maybe not exactly as we thought it would, but that's all right, too. To wake up in the morning and feel excited; to go to bed each night and feel reasonably content, this is possible when we get on the path from perfectionism to balance.

The glorious transformation comes from within when we are more accepting of our own humanity. When we become less self-critical, we will be more understanding of others. Habits, particularly old habits, are hard to change. But a warm heart is more important than a clean house. The outwardly perfect house could be one of denial. The controlling personality could actually be out of control inside.

Ask yourself some questions to get a better idea if you tend toward having perfectionist trait symptoms.

- Do you have difficulty letting others help you, feeling you can do everything better?
- Is neatness a priority over creativity?
- If someone breaks something in your house, is your immediate reaction to let the person know how much you loved the object, forgetting it was an accident?
- How upset do you get when you make a mistake? Are you overly hard on yourself?
- Are you able to do your best and let go, regardless of the outcome?
- What is your frustration level, day to day?
- If you're not in the mood to wash the pots and pans, would you ever leave them soaking in the sink until morning?
- When someone you love lets you down, do you ever admit that your expectations may have been unrealistically high?
- Do you feel self-conscious that you are not good enough and, as a result, withhold love from someone for fear that he or she will discover you're human?
- Do you feel guilty when you take time for a carefree moment when you are off limits, unavailable and having fun doing nothing?

- Is all your playtime highly organized, scheduled well in advance and always an "event"?
- Do you always find it difficult to leave work for later and take a break, in the office or at home?
- Do you become irritated if you are a guest in a home where the overall neatness does not meet your high standards?
- If you are not up to a social date, do you feel comfortable calling your friend and postponing, or do you feel the person is counting on you so much that you must go through with the motions?
- Are you overly competitive in a sport, such as tennis or golf, to the extent that you don't enjoy playing unless you win?

Many of you tell me your spouse is a perfectionist with demanding expectations. Maybe you have a mother-in-law or a mother who tends in this direction, or perhaps you have a child who strives to be perfect. Possibly you have a boss or employees who needs to readjust the balance in their lives.

No one of us is spared the need to figure out and then work out ways to bring our inner self and our outer self in harmony with the possibilities available to us.

The way to have more perfect moments is to feel free inside your soul, free from guilt, free from compulsions, free from frustrations and unnecessary anguish. When we clear up the imperfections in our thinking, in our actions, and in our core, the possibilities are all around us, all the time.

By giving up being a perfectionist, we can feel joy in life as it unfolds to us.

I think I have earned some credentials along the way to write this book. I've been a paid perfectionist for over thirty-five years. I'm hired to help create perfect rooms in perfect houses and make clients perfectly happy. In my failure to reach my goal, oddly enough, I feel joy, love, and freedom.

Just being ourselves, whoever that is, is not only good enough, it might be the secret to the divinity within each of us. Here is where we lose our insecurity, and here is where we feel an acceptance, a balance that makes us intuitively know we are on *our* path, we are on *our* way.

Here's to more perfect moments. Here's to focusing on the possible. Here's to balance and freedom.

With affection, appreciation, and admiration,

Alexandra Stoddard
Stonington Village, Connecticut

Yield and overcome;
Bend and be straight;
Empty and be full;
Wear out and be new;
Have little and gain;
Have much and be confused.

Therefore wise men embrace the one
And set an example to all.
Not putting on a display,
They shine forth.
Not justifying themselves,
They are distinguished.
Not boasting,
They receive recognition.
Not bragging,
They never falter.
They do not quarrel,
So no one quarrels with them.
Therefore the ancients say,
    "Yield and overcome."
Is that an empty saying?
Be really whole,
And all things will come to you.

LAO-TZU

The Art
of the Possible

PART ONE

Balancing
Expectations

1

Where Are You on Your Path?

Living in balance and purity is the
highest good for you and the earth.

—DR. DEEPAK CHOPRA

Perfectionism: A Life Out of Balance

A publisher once took me to lunch to ask me if I would write a book entitled *How to Have a Perfect Day.* I laughed and said, "I could never write that book. I've never had a perfect day. I don't believe it's possible, even though I've been a paid perfectionist for over thirty-five years."

Over the years, both in my personal and professional life, I've come to see too many people destroy themselves because they demand of themselves and the rest of the world, perfection: Home must always be clean and tidy, children must always be happy, and everything must be in order, always. We can indeed have moments of perfection. When we do, they lift us up and delight us. But if the focus is *perpetual* perfection, there is no peace. With perfection, there is always more to be done because perfection is an illusion, and it always eludes us no matter how hard we try. Some people can do nothing for fear they will not do it perfectly. When we are under the rule of perfection, we can no longer choose what is in our own best interest, we can no longer direct our own actions.

Why do we strive for perfection? Is it so that we can "be the best" and therefore receive affirmation from others? But what good will others' praise be if we have not figured out what makes us feel good about ourselves? To be able to live life as we want is a sign of earthly virtue. To be able to do good on earth, in our own unique way, being grounded, using our talents wisely, while enjoying the process, brings meaning to our lives. It is our birthright to be ourselves rather than to conform to others' ideas of how we should be. But how many of us are able to achieve this high personal calling?

Sometimes we strive for perfection because we believe others depend on us to be perfect. Some of us feel that we've lost control of our lives if we fall short of our own ideas of perfection. As a young mother, whenever my daughters, Alexandra or Brooke, were mad at me, grumpy, or bored, I immediately felt I was a bad mother. I'd always get upset when, in the middle of one of those magical days when everything hums along beautifully, a crisis suddenly erupted. *Boom.* I would become tense, anxious, frustrated. I'd grit my teeth and think, *Who needs this aggravation? Who wants anything or anyone to spoil a perfect day?* I'd feel loving and fine until I heard the girls screaming or fighting. Then I would immediately think, *I'm failing as a mother.*

The expectation of perfection can make us feel defeated, particularly when situations are beyond our control. Perfectionism does not take into account the uncertainties of life, the questions we cannot answer, the contradictions, the challenges of change. What is the meaning of life? How can we gain knowledge, truth, and love? What are we to strive for in our limited time on earth? Why must we get sick? Why do we suffer? Our greatest challenge in life is to understand how to cope with these uncertainties in our individual lives because we don't all have the same solutions to our deepest questions. As my spiritual sage John Bowen Coburn, religious leader and former Episcopalian bishop of Massachusetts who married Peter and me, says, we have to "relate to the ineffable. We have to open ourselves to the mystery of creation where we are." Each of us must face the unexplainable, the pain, the disappointment, and the grief and losses in our lives. Each one of us has to determine for ourselves how we shall live with the

He finds both wrong by being in extremes. He labors to plant his feet, to be the beam of the balance.

EMERSON

mysteries of existence, with the unanswered questions, and with reality, regardless of how uncomfortable it can be. We have to learn acceptance because whenever there is love there is potential loss.

The Dark Side of Perfectionism

Most of us are trying hard to improve our lives and the world around us. This is a healthy impulse that makes life far more pleasant day to day. But if we begin to think that we can make everything perfect, we become frantic and imbalanced. While perfectionistic strivings can often bring great results, we must look perfectionism in the face and see it for what it really is: a danger to our health, happiness, and success, which cuts us off from our higher purpose and goals.

As an interior designer, I've come face to face with many perfectionists who have tutored me on the dark side of this trait. When the inclination toward perfectionism becomes obsessive, we become driven by our narrow view of what is important. Perfectionism actually can be a form of self-protection, a way of trying to evade shortcomings by limiting attention to narrow, often shallow, areas of existence.

I do not know all the answers, I do not even know all the questions.

THEODOR REIK

Cynthia, an attractive young blond woman, once confessed to me that she couldn't sleep until everything in her apartment was in "perfect" order. Laundry had to be completed, ironing done, buttons sewn on, dishwasher empty, before she could go to sleep. She couldn't tolerate anything that seemed out of order, anywhere. Whenever she visited a friend's home and found the toilet paper roll inserted so that the paper rolled down from the back, not the front, she would reverse the roll to the "proper" way. She did this even at the department store public bathroom! Her perfectionism was like a grindstone continuously working away at her life. She couldn't just let matters be. As a result, there was no room in her life for spontaneity or pleasure; around every corner there was another insufferable problem to fix. Her driven course affected her life and it made others around her feel uneasy.

There is measure in everything. There are fixed limits beyond which and short of which right cannot find a resting place.

HORACE

Cynthia's behavior may sound extreme, but each of us has our own way of doing things and often we become irritated when something falls short of our personal standard. Switching toilet paper rolls from one side to the other doesn't make the world a better place. Nor does it improve our situation. This exaggerated intensity drains our vital energy and makes us less able to accomplish things that are worthwhile.

Perfectionism also causes constant anxiety. The perfectionist develops a proficiency in a few areas—a spic and span house, perfectly fitting clothes, a perfect figure—and feels inferior in every other area of life. A mother of three young boys once confessed to me that she had to give up using ironed linen napkins because life became "too much," and she had to be hospitalized for exhaustion. But she had learned something from her setback, she told me. She began to spend more time with her sons and found happiness there. "Now," she chuckled and said, "I use colorful cotton kitchen hand towels as napkins. They look great and they're easier to care for. They look just fine."

Perfectionism that goes too far causes rigidity, and, paradoxically, instability. The perfectionist is a person in crisis, and everyone around her feels driven away by her own discomfort with herself.

Perfectionism spells paralysis.

WINSTON CHURCHILL

Perfectionists may think other people should live

by their own impossible standards. I bristle when I sense that someone is trying to dominate me with his or her expectations. This is what happened in our families when Peter and I were first married. We were not the typical, perfect young newlyweds. We were real people with histories. I was thirty-two years old. I had two smart, adorable, loving, and well-adjusted young daughters from a previous marriage and Peter, whom I had known for over twenty years, had four children of his own plus two stepchildren, making a combined family of eight children. In addition to all the children, Peter was nineteen years older than I, which made family members speculate, doubt, and judge us. Some actively protested.

Becoming more and more aware of all that is possible moves your whole life into greater balance.

I was happy and excited by my career as an interior designer, and grateful that I had found someone so wonderful to love. To the perfectionists in our families, however, we were failures. We had baggage that made us ungainly and awkward, too large and too quirky. Perfectionists don't recognize the subjectivity of their own views. Doesn't everybody agree on what's right? Perfectionists who haven't been divorced feel superior to those who have. Perfectionists who have big homes feel superior to those who live in small apartments crammed with children. Perfectionists who have two sets of silver make certain to mention this fact to those who only have one or none. This kind of thinking kills life rather than enhances it. Our family hampered any connection Peter and I may have enjoyed with them because we didn't fit their ideas of perfection. Some members of his family nicknamed me "Little Alexandra," which I found offensive. More cruelly, some would routinely ask me if I had a separate bedroom for every child, since housing so many children seemed so absurd to them. The bottom line was, people like Peter and me didn't fit in.

All of us have our areas where we go overboard. The kitchen countertops in our New York apartment are two-inch butcher block. I love them when they're freshly sanded, grease free, pure, bare, and beautiful. But I also love chopping on them, preparing meals on them, and using them with joyous abandon, getting them greasy and dirty. I care about these smooth, bleached, maple surfaces. I also care about family and friends and being able to make these gorgeous surfaces useful to people's everyday enjoyment.

These counters are not zero maintenance. After cooking lots of meals, I pour boiling water on them and scrub them with Ajax or Comet cleanser. Once the counters are dry and I see where the grease is, I sand the counters smooth until the surface is uniform in color. Frankly, Formica wouldn't give me the same karma. They look so good that our kitchen doubles as a place to do company projects, because when we're not preparing meals, these areas are devoid of clutter. The Japanese saying "space to breathe" is soothing and true.

Caring needn't be a burden. If I love something, it is a joy to maintain. The key to knowing whether our little obsessions are healthy or not is whether we're having fun. If we complain about any area of our lives that involves material possessions, it's a signal we don't have the right balance. One way or another, we must learn to let go, downscale, or lower our standards just enough so we can manage to enjoy ourselves. There may be a persistent, pervasive, perfectionist in all of us. Being aware of your perfectionistic tendencies can help you to focus on all the joyful possibilities available to you throughout your life. Knowing what's possible, going for it, living each day with a sense of pleasure, is an art. We hone this art over a lifetime.

There's something woefully lacking in any fragmentary approach to life, however intriguing any single fragment happens to be.

DEEPAK CHOPRA

The Challenge of Balance

Balance, the middle path, is the key to a happy and purposeful life. It can be achieved only by letting go of perfectionism. Our very life, I've discovered, is an awesome balancing act. Rarely do people keep an even keel, maintaining equilibrium over a lifetime. Even though it may seem easy, moderation, we often find, is the most difficult path to follow. Even the most expert tightrope walker occasionally loses balance and falls.

What's come to perfection perishes.

ROBERT BROWNING

Although few of us have our lives in perpetual balance, we know that when we do, our minds and bodies are in equanimity. Our metabolism and hormones function as they should and our thoughts are constructive. Our sense of wholeness and contentment depends on our ability to harmonize these aspects of our life—mind, body, and spirit—within our own particular circumstances, doing the best we can under those conditions. Paradoxically, when we become aware that we need to strive for balance rather than for perfection, our possibilities for joy and peace become infinite.

There are very few human beings who receive the truth, complete and staggering, by instant illumination. Most of them acquire it fragment by fragment...

ANAÏS NIN

In order to realize this potential, we must become more realistic and focus on what's possible. By being more honest with ourselves, about our capabilities, we often find that we can go beyond ourselves. You have to have your feet on the ground in order to jump into the air. You also need to know that the ground will hold.

When I was touring the country promoting *Making Choices: The Joy of a Courageous Life,* I urged audiences to "buck up" to the challenge of difficult times. Some people told me they couldn't always be strong, even though that was what they wanted; there are times when the people I spoke with get the "black dog," feel blue, or become seriously depressed. Facing the challenge of life does not mean you will never feel defeated by it. Getting fired, losing a loved one, finding out that you or someone close to you have a serious illness are terrible things to have to face. We cannot respond to these afflictions with absolute strength. That is unrealistic. These situations are hard, sometimes devastatingly so. But if you face the facts, do what you can do and not expect the impossible, you will feel your own foundations holding firm even in crisis. Knowing who you are, both what gives you pleasure and what causes you pain, will prevent you from falling back too far. When you realistically focus on your own potential within your circumstances, you will have built a safety net to catch you when you fall. Gradually, you will feel more and more moments of pure joy. This will sustain you through the hard times.

Toleration. . .is the greatest gift of the mind; it requires the same effort of the brain that it takes to balance oneself on a bicycle.

HELEN KELLER

Sogyal Rinpoche speaks to this point in his spiritual classic *The Tibetan Book of Living and Dying*: "Our task is to strike a balance, to find a middle way, to learn not to overstretch ourselves with extraneous activities and preoccupations." Balance, I've found, is the key to a stable and fulfilled life.

Toward a New Way of Being

The search for balance might not seem dramatic or daring, but it does take courage. It means having trust that in the long term, the center will hold. We can maintain our health, manage stress, feel joy, love, and freedom only when we liberate ourselves from the tyranny of demanding perfection from ourselves and others.

Will balance provide us with a perfect life? No. We get sick. We lose loved ones. We lose jobs, and we lose love. Balance does not prevent the pain from entering our lives. But by understanding the power of balance, by knowing that we can meet our losses with gains, we can more gracefully come to terms with our death as well as our life, chaos as well as order, stillness as well as activity, pain as well as pleasure. This is the challenge of balance: to make our own way, even though things do not always work out as we wish.

What does it take for us to open ourselves to a balanced life? Though there is no one road map to a balanced life, on whatever road you take there will be lots of landmarks along the way. When we have compassion for ourselves and others, whenever we learn to accept our strengths as well as our limitations, we are headed in the right direction. When we aren't caring or sensitive enough to ourselves to set limits, we run off course and become self-pitying, anxious, and depressed. When our labors feel burdensome and our demands of ourselves become unforgiving, we have gone too far. People who set their course toward balance know that there is time to take it easy and to take the scenic route.

To know how to live is my trade and my art.
MICHEL DE MONTAIGNE

...and I tell myself that whoever says he has finished a painting is terribly arrogant. Finished means complete perfect, and I am working hard without moving ahead, searching, feeling my way without achieving much...
CLAUDE MONET

Simplifying Our Lives for Balance

Simplifying our lives is often a way to achieve balance. When we have less, often we can have more.

The other day, I was planting more ivy under the shade of one of the two maple trees in our backyard. "In such a small place you can have a more perfect garden. It's manageable," said Peter. When you have so little, everything you plant rises in importance. Some of the most humble, simple things in life turn out to be the most satisfying.

The Freedom to Be Imperfect

We can all try to improve whatever we do. One column I wrote for *McCall's* magazine was titled "How to Be a Good, Not Perfect, Parent." Good is good enough. Striving for perfection is okay, expecting it is not. You can give a perfect example but not necessarily *be* a perfect example. You (as I have in the past) can make a perfect tennis stroke, but not every time you rally. You can have a perfect moment. A rose blossom can be perfect. You can have a perfect bath or afternoon or salad. I've experienced a perfect meal in France with my love. But perfection is not continuous, any more than joy. You catch life on the fly; you can't cling to it but must let it flow through you. It's transparent, like the sun on your back. The secret is to completely appreciate the moment without trying to perfect it. Then perfection can be found anywhere. Like beauty, perfection is realized "in the eye of the beholder."

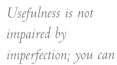

Usefulness is not impaired by imperfection; you can drink from a chipped cup.

GRETA K. NAGEL

One July morning, I had a wonderful experience of the freedom that comes with being able to balance success and failure. Some people from *House Beautiful* magazine were scheduled to photograph our cottage in Stonington for an article that was to appear in the magazine. I got the big idea to bleach and spray starch all the white dotted-swiss cotton curtains in the house before the shoot. It felt refreshing to scoop up the limp, yellowed pile and drop them off at our local Laundromat. There they soaked them in bleach overnight in order to get them sparkling white again. I love to iron, so it wasn't going to be a big effort to sort out which curtains belonged to which window, dampen them, roll up each set, spray starch them and, finally, hang them back up. But something happened that I hadn't counted on.

One soul is a counterpoise of all souls, as a capillary column of water is a balance for the sea.

EMERSON

I'd been out of town in Portland, Oregon, the week before, giving a seminar. A lot of my planning for the shoot was completed on the airplane. But the hands-on work was still to be done, and my schedule was filling up. Peter's sister's annual "cousins' day" was being held the weekend before the shoot. I was in one of my "can do" moods and decided to have a family Sunday lunch at our cottage after the reunion for all the out-of-towners. In my enthusiasm, I'd grabbed hold of more than I could handle. On our way back from the reunion, we picked up the curtains from the Laundromat. Each window in our cottage is a different height and width, and the curtains all look alike. I could see that the labels identifying which panel would fit in which window had vanished in the bleach.

We ran up and down the stairs and from room to room trying to figure out where everything went. It was impossible. We didn't know if we could stand the pressure. Mid-morning on Monday, we looked out a naked living room window and saw a van pull up to the house. Oh no! We panicked. Out of the van popped the energetic *House Beautiful* team. Holding the wrong curtain panels in each hand, we both looked at each other, and laughed. In the words of writer Jean Houston, "At the height of laughter, the universe is flung into a kaleidoscope of new possibilities."

Immediately, we draped the curtains over the back of the chair, dashed out to greet everyone, and helped them bring in their equipment. We confessed our situation to the decorating editor, my friend Carolyn Englefield, and she too laughed. "Oh, thank God, Alexandra, you're normal."

Reaching Our Potential Through Excellence

My friend and former boss Eleanor McMillen Brown founded one of the most respected design firms in New York. Mrs. Brown was known by everyone as a perfectionist. But over the years, I've come to understand what a highly attuned awareness and aesthetic she had, as well as a well developed sense of restraint. She understood the art of the possible. When a journalist questioned her on her ninety-fifth birthday about her sense of perfection she replied evenly, "When you live as long as I have and have experienced as much as I have, you come to understand that no one has 100 percent all the time. You do the best you can under the circumstances. Perfectionism builds, don't you think?"

Nature is an infinite sphere of which the center is everywhere and the circumference nowhere.

BLAISE PASCAL

The art of the possible requires intelligent compromise. We have to learn to give as well as take, to find solutions in situations when our first choices don't work. If you do your best and not expect everything to work out perfectly or even according to your original plan, in time, with focused energy, patience, and experience, you improve every aspect of your life. You can say, "Yes, perfection builds."

What all of us who were fortunate enough to be Eleanor Brown's protégés learned was more valuable than what her design skills and knowledge of history and decorative arts could teach us. We learned that through a love of beauty, order, symmetry, proportion, scale and, most of all, balance, excellence *is* possible.

*Life is the first gift,
love is the second, and
understanding, the third.*

MARGE PIERCY

We saw how she paced herself so she was able not only to achieve excellence but also to find pleasure in the process. Mrs. Brown clearly understood the difference between what was important and what was only superficial. Perfectionism distorts our ability to make this distinction. It obscures perspective. Artists know this; they learn through experience that when you keep working at a painting or a sculpture to try to "make it perfect," you may make it flat and miss the beauty that is already there, even in the imperfections. When we focus on perfection, we lose our good judgment and our freedom to choose.

*All things are literally
better, lovelier, and
more beloved for the
imperfections which
have been divinely
appointed...*

JOHN RUSKIN

Mrs. Brown exemplified values and ideas that continue to light my path when I question what the next step should be for me. What direction should I take as familiar doors close and I attempt to open new ones? Although she never imposed her views upon her staff, her example of excellence elevated our sights and understanding.

Mrs. Brown insisted we all leave the firm at five P.M. sharp, encouraging us to balance our work with recreation, culture, and fellowship. All through her eighties she entertained. She went to the theater and concerts. She attended cultural events, parties and lectures in the evenings. She maintained a balance between evenings home alone reading and doing desk work, nights out at a cultural event, and dining with friends in their apartments or at restaurants or at her home. What fueled her creative juices was also good for us. While every home had a television or two, there was an expectation that we would further stimulate ourselves by going to a gallery opening, attending a seminar, or taking a course. We looked at her, saw how she thrived, and wanted to take a page out of her book. As elegant as her dinner parties were, they were for no more than eight; they were simple and we all went home early in order to get a good night's sleep. She often reminded me that you have to always be in training in order to perform at your peak. We didn't have cocktail hour but instead were offered a refreshment before being seated for dinner. Without being rigid, her habits of excellence expanded us; they were never limiting.

The challenge to an individual to find his or her "crucial balance" is always there.

DR. JAY B. ROHRLICH

Mrs. Brown loved to walk to her appointments. Whenever we would meet, no matter how long her walk, she never appeared breathless, and she was always on time. By not over-extending herself, she was able to commit herself fully to everything she did, concentrating on the present so firmly that she never appeared scattered.

What Is Possible?

"The most meaningful thing you can live for is to reach your full potential," says Deepak Chopra in *Ageless Body, Timeless Mind.* "At any given age the body and mind you experience are but a tiny fraction of the possibilities still open to you—there are always infinite new skills, insights, and depths of realization ahead of you."

Falling short of perfection is a process that just never stops.

WILLIAM SHAWN

In my book *Living a Beautiful Life: 500 Ways to Add Elegance, Order, Beauty and Joy to Every Day of Your Life,* I focused on the 95 percent of our lives composed of daily rituals: cooking, cleaning, commuting, working, etc.: "Making the things you do every day as beautiful and pleasurable as possible is a way to live a happy life. Yet many of us don't seem to do this." In that opening sentence, I quite deliberately chose the word *possible*. By making all the little things—the details and rituals—a little better, we enrich our journey, nourish our soul, and deepen ourselves spiritually. Something as simple as grinding your coffee beans each morning; having a wind chime make music out of the breeze; keeping your favorite fruit glycerin soap at the kitchen sink or stacking colorful boxes in your office to hold some necessary files; moving the children's swings so you can watch them play from the kitchen window; placing a meditation bench in your yard; having a tea ceremony every day—are all within our reach. We enter and possess the place of the possible. We know we are there when we arrive.

Everything has its own opposite, and one cannot exist without the other. You can't know happiness without the idea of sorrow. So in everything in the universe—physical, moral or spiritual—there are two sides.

DR. DAVID EISENBERG

That book gave birth to *Grace Notes*, which illuminated the simple things we can do in our daily lives to help turn anything ordinary into a small epiphany: a moment in which we intuitively grasp the essential nature or meaning of life through something simple. It's not a matter of time, energy, or money to light a candle when we dine; say a blessing; have a flower on our writing desk; use our favorite glass for a refreshing drink; use a fountain pen when we write a note; change the tired buttons on an old coat to shiny brass ones or do something for a loved one without anyone knowing who did it. Such choices elevate all our moments, as though we're being lifted up by an invisible source. If we feel better about our lives as they unfold, doing what is in our reach to accomplish, we will indeed feel a subtle transformation of mind, body, and spirit. The small steps—the minor adjustments we make to improve the climate of our inner lives as well as the physical environment around us—have a direct affect on our mental and physical well-being.

Last fall, when on a book tour, I was having lunch with an old friend with whom I played the tennis circuit as a teenager. The other guest was a fascinating woman who owned an independent bookstore where I was giving a talk and signing books. The three of us seriously discussed the change in people's reading habits: Why do people read what they read? What do we expect to get from the pages of a book? Who is reading and what kinds of books are popular today? Few conversations interest me more than ones about the mystery of personal enlightenment and the power of the written word.

The purpose of life is wholeness, which engages every aspect of living into the harmony we can only find in balance.

We concluded that each of us wants to feel reasonably content when we go to sleep at night. We want to do the best we can under the circumstances, learn to let go and be calm, quiet, and at peace within ourselves. Each of us must discover that consciousness in our own way. Each of us has to find our own answers to life's deepest questions. One way can never be right for everyone, not in a family, a community, a country, or the world. My way may not be the same as yours. We can take comfort and insight from each other. But we cannot know what is best for anyone but ourselves. Nor is it possible for anyone else to know or understand what is best for us. We can find inspiration in literature, philosophy, religious teachings, and from healers and thinkers who have in some special way cast light on the human condition. But we must take what works for us and not feel manipulated by the rest. Our objective is to become comfortable being ourselves. I feel that there is a universal creative energy that each of us can tap into. We can use it as a resource and source of connection to each other. When

Whatever is flexible and loving will tend to grow, whatever is rigid and blocked will wither and die.

LAO-TZU

we explore this potential, we discover and rediscover what's possible for us each day we are alive.

When we experience this balanced sense of wisdom about our lives, we know it. At my husband Peter's fiftieth reunion at Yale, we were all on our way over to a reception at the Beinecke Library when the rain suddenly started to pour down. There I was, as usual, without an umbrella. (I'm such an optimist, I naively think the rain will fall at appropriate intervals when I'm in shelter. Whenever I carry one of my flower-strewn umbrellas it becomes a walking stick because it never rains.) Peter's classmate and friend John V. Lindsay, author, lawyer and a valiant former mayor of New York City, let me share his umbrella as we walked two blocks after the reception to Silliman College to the class of '44 dinner, which was being held under a tent.

John and I enjoy a mutual admiration that grew from the time his twin brother, David, died of cancer several years after Peter and I had married. How much can you share under an umbrella in the rain walking two short blocks to dinner? A lot. "Isn't it wonderful to be here, John?" I mused. With his customary grin he answered, "It is better than the alternative. It *is* better than the alternative." We both laughed in recognition. John has had several major heart operations. Being there, even in imperfect form, is surely better than the alternative. The drenching rain was so utterly insignificant in the big scheme of things. What was important was that we were alive and *there*. What mattered most was that we could recognize and appreciate that it is enough to have what is possible. If you've lost the ability to run because of a bad knee or bad back, you can still swim or walk. Acknowledging that we cannot always

Everybody thinks of changing humanity and nobody thinks of changing himself.

LEO TOLSTOY

control our lives allowed John and me to experience a moment of joy, love, and freedom in our friendship with each other.

Lowering Expectations to Raise Satisfaction

When I was younger, I felt urgency about life. I attended to everything as if it required immediate care. I was on twenty-four hour call for my family, my children and my work. Every project begun needed to be completed before I slept. My life was hectic because I condensed too much activity into too few hours and I expected to be able to do everything perfectly. To survive, I just tried harder, did more. Everything within my reach or grasp I felt obligated to fix, improve, mend, or make better. My all was not enough. I strongly felt I had to prove myself, to constantly justify my life. One day over lunch, seeing that I was frantic, my mother told me softly that the only thing I lacked was "confidence" in myself. I'm sure she was right; however, her expectations for me were boundless and I came to expect those things of myself, which caused me enormous strain.

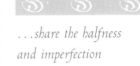

...share the halfness and imperfection of humanity.

EMERSON

I'll never forget the time she came to our tiny rent-controlled apartment and found gunk in the crack between the stove and the refrigerator. The space is just wide enough to accumulate soot, grease, and dust but not big enough to allow your hand in there to clean. My mother attached a rag to the end of a broom with elastic bands, soaked it in ammonia, and got to work. I stood by, horrified. I felt like a child with dirty underwear. While she was well-meaning and only try-

My joy, my grief, my hope, my love,/Did all within this circle move.

EDMUND WALLER

ing to help, it shattered me. Why couldn't she have focused on the gleaming waxed floors or the shiny brass railing of the stairs to our sunken living room? Even the windows were clean. I realized that afternoon that one of the reasons we lack confidence is because unattainable standards are put on us.

Recently, we replaced our vintage Westinghouse refrigerator with a new model. The old one was worn out. The grille on the bottom of the machine always rested on the floor of the kitchen because the hooks that held it in place had broken off. Every time I tried to attach it, I saw that same ugly sight of disgusting dirt and sludge—there, but hidden if only the grille could be attached. The lingering memory of my mother cleaning between the cracks in my old apartment came to mind every time I tried to kick that grille back into place. I'm grateful that Mother wasn't around to see *that* horror. Even *I* was appalled when I saw the junk behind the old refrigerator when it was carted away.

The hero of my tale, whom I love with all the power of my soul, whom I have tried to portray in all his beauty, who has been, is, and will be beautiful, is Truth.

LEO TOLSTOY

Sometimes it's hard to cope; it's difficult to keep all the balls in the air. We all get pretty caught up in our family, the demands of society, our work, and the pressures of mere survival. Though I can understand the necessity for stacking more dishes, doing another load of laundry, buying more groceries, cooking another meal, driving children around in traffic, changing the sheets, paying the bills, and mowing the lawn, whenever you expect too much, the angst and frustration of pushing too hard causes too much stress, and you lose your balance. The full rich life can also become a very harried one.

In our family we talk about lowering our "E," which literally raises our "S." By lowering our expectations, not our standards, we become more realistic about what we can accomplish while still encouraging ourselves to do our best. In the end, we are more satisfied. The satisfaction comes from knowing when to let go and not attempt to obtain perfection. Letting go enhances our pleasure in the process of doing and being. Human beings have real limits. We can stretch ourselves, reach high and far, live life with our full force, but in the end, we must come face-to-face with our very human limitations. It is up to each of us to discover and accept our own limits even as we focus on living well. And I've discovered that living well is very good indeed.

Living...like studying, needs a little practice.

OCTAVIA WALDO

I'm reminded of this simple, but not easy, truth whenever I think back on my brief riding and my tennis playing days. My mother loved horses and became an accomplished rider, winning fifty-nine medals in Madison Square Garden for her equestrian performance. Our family joined a small hunt club in Connecticut; all four children took riding lessons from the masterly Raymond Burr. Mother's hopes were high that one of us would make the national equestrian team. But alas, none of us even qualified to ride in the annual horse show. I felt so sorry for the horse and the rider as the jumps got higher, deeper, and more dangerous. I didn't have the knack for serious horsemanship. For me—like professional singing—it wasn't possible.

My nonriding friends cynically warned me that riding gave you a big rear end anyway, so I took to the swimming pool and cooled off, relieved to be free from the horse flies. Dressed in tennis whites, I took to the courts, only to learn that every game has a way of judging and signaling how you are doing. After years of lessons and practice, and by both losing and sometimes winning, I realized that almost all my shots hugged the net. I loved hitting a low ball that would tick the net as it whizzed low into my opponent's court. I learned that by leaning forward ever so

You have to accept whatever comes and the only important thing is that you meet it with courage and with the best that you have to give.

ELEANOR ROOSEVELT

slightly, perhaps 10 percent more, a larger number of those shots got over the net with increasing speed. By allowing myself to see what I was doing right and what I was doing wrong, I was able to sharpen my game. The difference between winning and losing was far closer than I imagined.

Ne quid nimus.
(Nothing in excess.)

MOTTO

We can all tune up our skills by focusing more attention on our strengths rather than dwelling on our weaknesses. Tennis taught me to play the game, win or lose. If I'd had expectations of always winning, I'd forever be disappointed, or I'd have to play with a dreadfully poor opponent which would, as a pattern, be hopelessly boring. Instead, I focused on hitting a good stroke. I played the game. I was there, win or lose. I've never once played a perfect game, but I've had perfect moments. There were moments when my backhand crosscourt shot was beautiful, when I'd lean into it, putting such a topspin on the ball with a wide angle that it would win the point. Occasionally, like the golfer's hole in one, I'd actually hit a perfect shot. I will remember those days.

Life is so made that
opposites sway about
a trembling center
of balance.

D. H. LAWRENCE

Now, simply recalling the joy I experienced playing tennis for thirty-five years brings me pleasure. Because of my tricky back, I can no longer play. I loved every moment on the court. Now, I've let go; I am no longer a tennis player. Nothing lasts forever. We have to learn how to let go whether we want to or not. But whenever we let go, we actually gain something. We realize that when we close a door, another one opens. The secret is to live each chapter of our lives fully, so that when our story ends we don't have longing and regrets.

Life presses on. We must catch the joy and do what's possible here and now. We can't single-handedly make the world or ourselves perfect. We don't have perfect parents, spouses, children, friends, neighbors, coworkers, spiritual guides, or mentors. But we have the gift of life. We can make the best of every situation, we can trust our intuition, take risks, extend ourselves, try new things, reach out to others in loving ways, and lower our expectations, our false impressions that perfection is always attainable. Since I've trained myself to lower my "E," my "S"—satisfactions—have increased tenfold.

We are human, we make mistakes. We leave things undone that we should do. We aren't always ready at the starting gate. We miss the boat. We let ourselves and others down. We get sick. But I believe we are all, in our own ways, doing the best we can at the time, even if we may not be at our best. We must try to be more tolerant of ourselves. When we are, we will become more understanding of others. When we step back from perfection, we step toward humanity. We become more understanding, more empathetic. This alone greatly reduces anxiety and our sense of frustration about things we can't control. The plumber will come, but not necessarily on time. The curtains will look fresh and clean, but they will never be as white as they were when they were brand new. All you have to do to learn how not to be a perfectionist is to live in an old house. Peter and I have grown to relax and appreciate the irregularities, the idiosyncrasies, the sheer quirkiness of our old cottage.

Simply be aware of the oneness of things.

LAO-TZU

The more I have been able to limit my expectations, the more I enjoy life. By letting go I have also grown more understanding and tolerant of the enormous complexities of the human soul that make life so unpredictable. As my friend John Coburn often says when speaking about the uncertainties of life, "You never know." Learning this over these past several years has brought me far more serenity and pleasure than in all the years before. I no longer strive for the impossible. I always "aim for the stars" and encourage myself to do my best, but I set realistic and attainable goals.

I owe this feeling of contentment to a combination of factors. Certainly, my maturing had something to do with my ability to know what's really important. Many of the dreams and goals I had in the past have found resolutions that satisfy and bring me pleasure. But I believe that I now truly understand the powerful tool of learning to let go. It is not possible to have any peace or freedom when we feel we must control everything and everybody, and when even an unmade bed and a sinkful of dishes can ruin our day. Through my interest in Eastern philosophy, I've learned to be more accepting, more realistic, and less demanding of myself and others.

In *Creating a Beautiful Home*, I shared what I had learned over the years about how counterproductive it is to be a perfectionist. Peter's and my experience of taking a wreck of an eighteenth-century cottage and slowly transforming it into a home was a revelation. That labor of love also became an act of forgiveness. We learned to accept and respect the house for all its imperfections. The charm, we discovered, comes from the funny unexpected angles, the warped floorboards, the irregularities, the uneven layers of paint. We were lucky to find such an old house. It is a simple house and was unappreciated by potential buyers for its authentic character and history. Everyone who walked through the front door must have turned up their noses at every awkward, humble detail.

We love our cottage even though it is far from perfect. We like it just the way it is—honest, authentic, relaxed, informal,

Living is a form of not being sure, not knowing what next or how. The moment you know how, you begin to die a little. The artist never entirely knows. We guess. We may be wrong, but we take leap after leap in the dark.

AGNES DE MILLE

comfortable, and Shaker plain. The happiest times in my adult life are enjoyed there. I feel completely free to let my hair down and kick up my heels in joyous amusement. I feel peaceful there.

We also delight in our cottage for its character. It has soul. The wide golden floorboards are ridiculously uneven. Our tiny hall off the living room is more like a ramp leading to the bathroom. The old windows swell up in the summer. I spend hours shaving them down so they can open wide to the sea air. A few panes of glass are cracked, but it's old bubbly glass, so we leave them as they are.

When Peter and I decided to buy our cottage and fix it up, we envisioned it as a place where we could settle in and retreat in order to write. But it didn't work out that way and instead, we found a new source of joy. We discovered the pleasures of working on an old house, caring for it, and attending to small details that make a big difference. I'm certain that if I didn't love it so much I would be less distracted from my writing. But here is a perfect little example of how thwarted expectations become new opportunities. The little joys are endless to we who have been apartment dwellers too long.

If you aspire to the highest place it is no disgrace to stop at the second, or even the third.

CICERO

We love running up and down the staircase. Whenever one of us is upstairs and someone climbs the stairs, we say, "Hey, hey, ho, ho." I had no idea why we did this. One day I discovered these words in Shakespeare's *Twelfth Night*: "A great while ago the world begun,/With hey, ho, the wind and the rain." It seemed a fitting connection, a celebration of what cannot be tamed. We couldn't tame our little cottage. It had to be itself, just as we must.

Why Focus on Perfection When You Can Have What Is Possible?

What do you really want from this gift of life? We're given this brief opportunity to let the light shine in as we give back whatever gifts we have. How can we best express our love and appreciation? I've learned to believe in balance as one of the most important life skills. We should try, but not push; care, but not smother; love, but not possess. Balance works. It centers us, makes us stable, allows us to be composed, and will teach us the many virtues of moderation. We cannot live a free life without extricating ourselves from excessive, blinding compulsions.

What are the circumstances that nourish some people to do well with their time on earth, while others die with dreams unrequited, love unconsummated, friendships unmade? What can we do to redirect ourselves so we begin to concentrate on what *is* possible rather than complaining about what is clearly out of our reach?

We're here on earth to play our part. Those pilgrims who paved our way and the saintly souls who have struggled with poverty and need were all witnesses to the pains, not the perfections, of the human condition. There is a great deal of misery in the world. There are and will continue to be situations that will challenge *all* our resources. We're all going to have to make sacrifices whether we want to or not. By being willing to confront reality, accepting what we can do and not pining for what is not in our stars, we can have the chance to travel the path to living well.

The more deeply I love life, the better I see the

I tore myself away from the safe comfort of certainties through my love for truth; and truth rewarded me.

SIMONE DE BEAUVOIR

big picture. If my life is of importance to anyone, it will be because I am living what is possible for me, flowing into new situations, striving and trying to make things work out as best as possible. But ultimately, by letting go, by freeing myself of the bad habit of doing too much or of wanting more than I need, I come back to myself and feel grounded. All I can attempt to do is be honest with myself as I explore the possibilities for my life in ever-changing situations.

We are involved in a life that passes understanding and our highest business is our daily life.

JOHN CAGE

And while I expect a great deal from myself and from others, from life and events, I increasingly know from life's experiences that I have to learn to accept loss. This is possible, but only if we change our attitude, unlearn much of what we've been brainwashed to believe, and learn to let go, feeling that calm peacefulness at our center. No one lives it all or dies with it all.

Loss is one area in life over which we have no control. Life is a continuous balancing of love and loss, because in order to have any loss mean something, we first have to have something we truly value.

My losses that come to mind are all close to home. I immediately recall my father. My father simply wasn't around much. To me, it was a lost opportunity not to have had a really close bond with him before he died.

My younger brother's suicide left a hole, and recently, my older brother died at fifty-seven from a massive stroke during open heart surgery. I now have one living sibling who is fifteen months older than I. My sister and I have been separated most of our adult lives due, I believe, to a mutual loss of trust and confidence. This discomforting relationship is especially painful and disappointing because so many sisters are best friends.

I have also experienced the hurtful loss resulting from the

cruel betrayal of a friend. I made the honest mistake of comparing this false friend to a true friend whom I had lost to cancer a few years before.

...humanism and the spirit of reasonableness are associated with the sense of humor and the sense of proportion...

LIN YUTANG

After my older brother, Powell, died, my spiritual sage John Coburn wrote me to share his wisdom about loss. "So times of loss are often especially times of love," John explained. "Memories are sharpened—and especially when sadness (or tragedy) comes, the awakening of memories can be very strengthening."

Some feelings of loss are from the disappointment of what might have been, while others are the piercing realities of what you once had and no longer have, how much you loved and cared for someone who, for some reason, is now gone despite your devotion.

I'm comforted to have my losses remedied by loving memories, loving family and friends. I've had to understand that fate is not in my hands. Often, all I can do is be present, to accept the truth, and learn how to grow in love and faith.

Sometimes I've been able to do something to help, and other times all I can do is send out loving energy. Our greatest losses are the ones that teach us how much we really love life, how much we care, and how deeply we're capable of loving another human soul.

What do you wish for in the time you have left? Do you want to be a part of something far greater than your own existence? How do you connect with others? What gifts and talents do you wish to pass on in hopes of becoming useful to generations not yet born? How do we begin from here?

2

Work
and
Money

When you love your work and do
a good job, the money follows.

—ELEANOR MCMILLEN BROWN

Satisfaction with the Sweat of Our Brow

Work holds a powerful place in each of our lives. We depend on it not only to survive, but to thrive. When our work life is not in balance, we suffer.

When we're good at what we do, we feel tremendous satisfaction and pleasure. It is in the process of doing, the act itself, that we feel most alive and vital. In his wise collection of classic stories and own commentary, *The Book of Virtues*, William Bennett speaks to the significance of work:

> Work is applied effort; it is whatever we put ourselves into, whatever we expend our energy on for the sake of accomplishing or achieving something. [Happiness in work comes] in doing things that one can take pride in doing well, and hence that one can *enjoy* doing. Those who have missed the joy of work, or of a job well done, have missed something very important.

Taking strength and pleasure from the work we do is critical to our happiness, security, and emotional stability. But finding the right work, staying vital and interested on the job, and knowing how to make changes when work becomes overwhelming is not always possible. These are challenges we all must face, often at several different points in our working lives. This can happen for one of two reasons: Either we become anxious and strained by doing too much work, or we become bored or apathetic by doing too little of what challenges us. When this happens, we have a hard time keeping our needs and our priorities in perspective. When we have a good job we may, out of fear of losing it or out of a compulsion to be the best, not know how to stop overworking. Or if we have a job we don't like, we may ignore opportunities for challenge or pleasure that may indeed be there within the job itself or the company.

After years and years of decorating, which I loved, I felt I wasn't challenging myself enough. I wrote about design and decoration, which stimulated me enormously but still, something was missing. Fortunately, I had a lucky break. The Birmingham Museum of Art in Alabama invited me to give a decorative arts lecture. Without hesitating, I accepted. I got off the telephone, nervously realizing I'd never before given a lecture on anything. How did I know I could? What if I suffered from stage fright and fainted at the podium? What would I say? It's one thing to be in someone's living room, sipping tea and discussing interior design with an eager client. But in front of a large audience? Who would attend my talk?

I never did anything worth doing by accident, nor did any of my inventions come by accident; they came by work.

THOMAS EDISON

I knew it wasn't possible to continue my design work without stretching myself further. After all, how many walls had I arranged to have knocked down, how many bathrooms and kitchens had I designed? It got so I could fairly easily figure out the puzzle, determine what needed to be done, and plan how to make that happen. My "juices" were no longer involved, and when this happens, you cannot go to the next level. I wanted my work to continue to be a thrilling adventure.

I paced up and down my office. Yes. I knew I was ready. Maybe I just needed a push. I thought back to all the people who I'd seen lecture well. Help! They all knew what they were talking about. Did I?

I confronted the challenge head on. Being married to a trial lawyer, I'm aware that it is impossible to be overly prepared. There is no substitute for knowing your material. And there is no substitute for passion. Would I be too nervous to project my excitement about the decoration of houses and matters of taste, style, and form?

Now, after thirty-plus years and hundreds and hundreds of opportunities to lecture, teach, and participate in seminars, I'm aware that this added dimension was essential to balance my career. I needed to expand beyond one-on-one work with clients. When you are with a live audience, you receive their energy. You feel their electrical charges. They tell you what they care about and ask your advice. All these years later, I still feel the excitement, every time. When I don't, I'll be ready to grow further. Everything I do in my career fuels the same flame. My talks increase my appreciation of the hands-on work. If I deserted my decorating roots, not only would I miss my clients and the need to dream up solutions to problems on the spot; I'd miss the workmen and workwomen. They're the ones who turn pipe dreams into practical, down-to-earth reality.

All experience is an arch to build up.

HENRY BROOKS ADAMS

As I was struggling to invent new stimulation in my work, I began to write about design. It was really this need to grow that turned me to the pen. I also designed some textiles, wallpaper, rugs, and furniture. If something wasn't available, we'd have it custom made. You may not be aware at the time of what you're building, but when you challenge yourself, doing much more than what's expected to learn new skills, you always feel more satisfaction in your work.

Sarah Stegner, the chef at the Ritz-Carlton Hotel in Chicago and the winner of the Beard prize for "the most promising chef

of the year" (1994), told me she is not a perfectionist. "I do my best," she said. "Every day I create a new
recipe or menu. In a year, that adds up."

Our work may not be what we want to do for the
rest of our lives, but it pays the bills now. We all have
periods when we merely coast. But in any work there
are usually hidden opportunities for advancement,
either direct or indirect. If you focus on what is possible under your own circumstances, letting go of the notion of
having "the perfect job," you may be able to discover what is
best for you given the opportunities available.

*All work is as seed
sown; it grows and
spreads, and sows
itself anew.*

THOMAS CARLYLE

Why Do People Dislike Work?

Many people feel about work the way we feel about paying taxes:
You gotta do it. Most of us work because we have to. We hope
that the work will fulfill us in some way, but essentially, we work
to pay the bills. When this is the whole story, work can become
drudgery. Work can begin to feel like only a burden and a terrible routine in which we experience all our efforts as futile. We
don't taste any satisfying fruit of our labor. Like Sisyphus in the
Greek myth, sometimes it seems as if our task is to roll a great
boulder up a mountain only to watch it roll down over and over
again.

One major reason why people dislike their work may be that
the work doesn't suit their emotional, spiritual, educational, or
intellectual needs and abilities. You love to be outdoors, but you
have a job working in a factory or a store. You may love to read
books and write stories, but you're a lawyer and your grueling
schedule allows you no time. Or you may love to spend time

with children, but you have a job working on Wall Street instead.

You may also dislike work because you are no longer doing what you set out to do or are no longer interested in what you're doing. Perhaps your job has grown in ways that take you away from what first gave you pleasure in it. You may have loved to cook and started a catering business to utilize your skills and enthusiasm. But over the years, you became so good at it that you went from chef to manager, and before you knew it, you were no longer cooking or even seeing the food you so loved to be around; now you're only administering to others.

When I go into my garden with a spade, and dig a bed, I feel such an exhilaration and health that I discover that I have been defrauding myself all this time in letting others do for me what I should have done with my own hands.

EMERSON

There are also many people who really love the kind of work they do but are stuck at the wrong company at a lower level than they'd like to be. You can get stuck if you haven't developed the skills to move on or if other opportunities are not available at your level of training. It is not always possible to find the particular job that perfectly suits your temperament and talents. If you live in a small town or need to acquire some new job skills, you may only have limited options.

A good job can also be ruined by coworkers and bosses who don't appreciate your contributions. Working for a brilliant yet tyrannical boss is enough to drive you into a constant state of anxiety. Yet, you may not have any other option at the present time because you haven't developed the skills to move to another position.

Some people feel superior to their work and therefore think they're unhappy working. Many young people who excelled in college and graduate school feel they are too good for the work they start out doing. Faxing, filing, and photocopying seems to them a waste of their education. They have not yet learned the wisdom of applying the same resolve to work that they did to their education. Getting the job done, whatever the assignment, is the most essential ingredient not only to doing good work, but eventually to getting good work. If someone hands me a Xerox copy with the edges cut off so that I cannot even read it, no academic degree in the world will convince me that that person can do a good job at any level.

Though they are unpleasant and frustrating, many of these problems can be alleviated. If you focus on the possible, you will see that you have the power to change your circumstances by taking some action. If you're unhappy with your job, the first thing you should do is put your résumé together. If you have a difficult time starting—many people are nervous or have difficulty working on a résumé—there are résumé writing services available in most cities. If you're not entirely sure that leaving will be possible—or what you really want to do—take another look at your job. Can you be making more positive connections with your coworkers? By reaching out to others, you will feel a sense of community. You will also see that you and your coworkers are an essential part of something bigger than yourselves. You can also support one another and affirm one another's work. Feeling integral is an important way to find meaning in work and is one of the main sources of satisfaction reported by people who enjoy their work.

Artists who seek perfection in everything are those who cannot attain it in anything.

EUGÈNE DELACROIX

Mrs. Brown considered her employees her family. We all cared about one another, and as a result, we worked in harmony together. The designers drew up the decorators' floor plans. The switchboard operator connected us to our clients. The shipping clerk mailed out our packages and took care of our inventory. When you think of how many different people work on a project, each with his or her own point of view as well as special training or a specific job to do, you understand the value of a caring atmosphere at work. It not only reduces pressure, but it also increases the sense of pride and pleasure in the process. You can't be a loner when you're part of a team. I've experienced stress in companies where everyone feels they're doing their own thing when, in fact, they're limiting their possibilities by not collaborating with their coworkers. Sharing ideas has a way of balancing things out. Rather than wanting credit for an idea, give it freely. You never know when you'll feel dried up and want to seek advice from a colleague.

We're all in this together. Wherever our job is, there is an opportunity to learn about lives of the people who work with you, away from the work environment.

As a lawyer in a large firm, Peter made an effort to get to know new associates by having lunch with one each week, on a regular basis. They'd eat in the company cafeteria, which wasn't more expensive than if each had eaten lunch alone. After twenty-six years of practicing this ritual, Peter made lasting friendships with the younger lawyers which continue today, even though he's left the firm.

Learning about the life behind the person at work adds so much rich texture to your journey. One of the bookkeepers at Mrs. Brown's decorating firm kept track of all birthdays, anniversaries, and births. In the fourteen-plus years that I worked at the firm, I'd always receive a card with a fresh flower on my desk to let me know I was remembered on a special day.

All the years I worked for companies before starting my own I made a point of leaving the office building each day and hav-

Joy and happiness are the concomitants of productive lives.

ERICH FROMM

A small daily task, if it be really daily, will beat the labors of a spasmodic Hercules.

ANTHONY TROLLOPE

ing a real lunch break. Lunch hour is yours. Having a banana and some instant coffee at your desk while making business calls can make you resent your workload. I know someone who worked like a dog, never taking a break and always eating lunch at his desk. He ended up with a ruptured ulcer. No one wants us to overdo. One of the lessons I've learned as a writer is that once you're in the flow, even when you take a break, your mind will continue to work even when you don't. I've learned to walk away from my pen and paper and have a lunch break.

When I was in my early twenties and free of parental responsibilities, I'd often go to a museum café for lunch with a friend. If I needed to be alone, I'd wander around a museum or art supply store, or go to a church and light a candle. New York offers such spice; merely stepping out onto the sidewalk offers a parade worth observing. But even if you work in a rural area, leaving the building and getting some

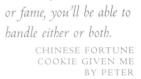

Whether you choose love or fame, you'll be able to handle either or both.
CHINESE FORTUNE
COOKIE GIVEN ME
BY PETER

fresh air is renewing. This minibreak, when taken regularly, is really an opportunity for you to appreciate your job more. And if you can, have lunch with someone you work with. No matter how modest your meal, you will return to your work with a refreshing awareness of your potential contribution to the whole. Caring for yourself and others has a way of rubbing off on your work.

Once I had children, I used this time to be with them for lunch, put them down for their naps, pick them up from school, and play with them. I was fortunate to live near my work. But whatever we do, we should find out what's possible in order to make the most out of our job situation.

Make extra efforts. Challenge yourself. Take every opportunity you can to achieve excellence and fulfillment. Make suggestions for improvement, and try following them yourself. Set goals. You'll be surprised how much that effort will, in return, deliver satisfaction to you.

Try to make your office or the area in which you work more your own. Bring in a beautiful lamp; buy a vase for your office and remember to bring in fresh flowers; hang up posters and pictures that reflect your passions and pleasures.

It is a bad plan that admits of no modification.

PUBLILIUS SYRUS

Recently I went to visit my daughter Brooke's work area at *Harper's Bazaar.* I was struck by the color and beauty of her space. She had covered a bulletin board with a chintz fabric with crisscrosses of ribbons so she could stick in family photographs, pictures that inspire her from magazines, postcards, invitations, quotations. This collage is alive, pulsating with images, information, and innovations.

Keep a pair of mugs or teacups and saucers at your office so you can take a minibreak with a business associate or coworker. Have a canister with an assortment of different kinds of tea bags so each person gets to pick according to taste and mood.

Let us, then, be up and doing/ With a heart for any fate;/ Still achieving, still pursuing,/ Learn to labor and to wait.

HENRY WADSWORTH LONGFELLOW

Make a deliberate effort to bring colorful touches to your work. Even if you have to spend your own money to have colored paper clips, file folders, and mailing envelopes, the cheer these small touches will bring you outweigh any minor costs. Browse in art supply stores for colorful elastic bands, colored pencils, felt-tip markers, and pens. Buy a fresh yellow, blue, or red blotter for your desk. This may be the best investment you can make for under two dollars. The more technical equipment we use, the more the need to counterbalance it with personal touches. Even scissors and tape dispensers can be yellow, pink, blue, or green. Buy a brightly colored clipboard. In an art supply store you can purchase an array of different hues of eight-by-ten-inch paper on which to write your "to-do" lists. When you make your work place warm and personal, you will find you'll look forward to being there.

Take breaks and do something you enjoy, even if it's only for ten minutes at a time. Spend some of those breaks alone, in solitude, if you can. These can be your meditation breaks when you quiet and relax your mind. If you have no opportunities or space to be alone at work, try taking a short walk outside. There is a healing power in these minutes of solitude.

...the love that goes out into our work comes back as love of self.

THOMAS MOORE

Remember that in any kind of work there will always be disappointments. Whether you raise children, publish books, run a university, teach first grade, or run a shop, even when you love your work, it will never be perfect sailing. People go on a sailboat for pleasure, but the sailor can't control the weather. I've never met anyone who can.

Money: Less Is Often More

We may also grow to dislike our work when we're only doing it for the money or when we're constantly worrying about it. Certainly we need the money. That is not in question. But when money becomes the beginning and end of our work, satisfaction falls by the wayside and eventually, we feel tyrannized by our job.

There are no secrets to success. It is the result of preparation, hard work, learning from failure.

GENERAL COLIN L. POWELL

When Tom and Marilyn bought an old farmhouse in Connecticut, they were both commuting to work in New York five days a week. But when their first child, Emily, was born, they both quit their pressured jobs. Tom was an investment advisor for a large Wall Street firm and Marilyn was an editor of a women's magazine. Both had saved enough money to give them a period of grace while they spent time with Emily and adjusted to their new lifestyle. By choosing to freelance, both from their Connecticut home, not only did they discover a far greater quality in their relationship to each other, but they were able to jointly parent Emily.

Our privileges can be no greater than our obligations. The protection of our rights can endure no longer than the performance of our responsibilities.

JOHN F. KENNEDY

Marilyn writes for women's magazines and she's also in the process of writing a book. Tom has private clients he helps on a consulting basis. He also writes for investment publications. Tom and Marilyn love their scaled-down lifestyle. Their needs are fewer. Because they no longer commute to New York five days a week, they don't need as many clothes, they save on travel expenses, and they don't need any child care because either Marilyn or Tom is always home to care for Emily.

Whenever we feel content in our lives, money is not out of balance in our priorities. We come to discover that by needing less, we have more. Tom and Marilyn now grow their own vegetables, raise chickens, do canning for the winter months, and reap great rewards from their commitment to simplifying their lives. When you're happy, you don't have anything to prove to anyone, not even yourself.

Karl was an internationally respected art expert for a major auction house, earning $175,000 a year, plus perks. He lectured all over America and Europe, was wined and dined by the rich and powerful, and was put up in luxury hotels as well as grand private estates. While on a family vacation in Maine, away from the wealth, the emphasis on materialism and money, Karl and Brenda took long walks on the beach and talked long after sunset. Both agreed something essential was missing in their lives. Karl rarely saw the children. He and Brenda had lost their closeness. They knew that a radical shift was required in order to move toward a more centered lifestyle. They agreed as partners that he would quit his job and they would both go back to teaching. Brenda used to teach sixth grade English but quit because Karl earned more than enough money in his job. But she missed her students. "I loved teaching. I can't understand how I could have quit." They decided to leave Chicago and move to a small town where the schools were good, not only for their teaching but also for their children.

...he who attempts to do all will waste his life in doing little.

SAMUEL JOHNSON

An international journalist living in London was miserable trying to cope with what she describes as gender discrimination. "Because I'm a woman, I was not given the same caliber of assignments as the male writers." For whatever reasons, this woman was unhappy even though she was paid well and equal to the men she worked with. She quit and now works for a not-for-profit environmental firm writing proposals for conservation projects around the world. While she earns half as much pay, her spirits have never been better. "I didn't know how wonderful a job environment could be. I work so much of my life. Because I'm single, this atmosphere is especially refreshing because I'm able to relax and be myself. Even after working long hours, I'm in the mood to see friends in the evening. It's a different kind of tired. I now feel the pleasure of work without the frustration and stress."

The great depend on their heart, not on their purse.

EMERSON

Peter and I met an attractive couple who left San Francisco and their high-paying jobs there in search of a more balanced life together. Bruce was a lawyer and Nancy ran a highly successful antique shop. They sold their town house and bought a house with some land in Napa Valley, where they now run a winery. It's small, but they love it. They travel together promoting their wines. On a recent trip to New York, they came up to our apartment for a visit. They were joyful about so many top restaurants now selling their wines. This couple feels very fortunate that they made the decision to completely change their lifestyle because it has strengthened their relationship. "We both work extremely hard and because we're together, we have empathy for each other, we understand what each of us feels."

The man who makes no mistakes does not usually make anything.

E. J. PHELPS

A reader recently sent me a letter telling me she's decided to change careers. "At forty, I'm quitting my job as a computer programmer and I've decided to become an interior designer. I've always wanted to use my aesthetic skills, and on my birthday, I realized I'm mature enough to know what's best for me. I'm really excited."

Money is often only a symbol of something else. We use money sometimes to present a good face to others, even though our spirits may be poor. Many wealthy people are among the most spiritually bankrupt. They bank on money to bring them contentment, and when that fails, they have no other resources.

There is nothing spiritual or noble about money. It is a tool, a necessity. We can enjoy money and see it indeed as the fruit of our labor. But there must be a balance between what your financial needs are and how hard you have to work to achieve that goal. We can certainly feel more control over our lives when we are financially secure. But no amount of money guarantees everything. Money certainly doesn't assure happiness. To anyone who has plenty of it, it is no big deal. But when we feel we don't have enough (when perhaps we do), we spend all our time trying to get more of it. Earning a lot of money at the expense of your peace does not make for a good economy of happiness. Once we let go of our preoccupation with money, we can let go of the superficial drives that distract us from our deeper desires.

Take a careful look at how much money you believe you "need." It may be less than you think. As my friend and literary agent Carl Brandt says, "Just because you can, doesn't necessarily mean you should." If you're willing to scale back, it may free you to do more to find satisfaction in your work. You may be able to do more things yourself in your home and save money. When I spend time doing something to improve our home, I'm not only saving money, I appreciate our home more. By expecting less and simplifying our lives, it becomes possible to live a more positive, peaceful life. How much do you need to live a good life? Take a look at what you have; do you really need it all? By focusing on questions like this, you can bring your money concerns into better perspective and better balance.

A year ago, I was invited to go into a business venture. The proposal was quite enticing. To help me think things through, Peter and Carl joined me for lunch. While waiting for our grilled swordfish to come, Carl raised the famous inquiry: "I guess you have to ask yourself what you want to be doing in five years." Peter and I looked at each other and both answered, "Exactly what we're doing now." The swordfish was delicious. I'd made up my mind. When we all left Carl said, "I'm really proud of you." I was proud of myself. I work hard enough. My life has a nice balance to it the way things are. Carl assured me, "You may not ever be rich, but you'll always eat."

Work-addicted people remain perfectionistic, and they fruitlessly persist in their obsessions with mastery and control. They experience imperfection, Elliot Jacques notes, "as bitter, persecuting failure." They cannot transcend imperfection by accepting it; instead, they feel defeated by it.

DR. JAY B. ROHRLICH

Knowing When to Stop

At a party recently, I had an interesting conversation with a film producer. We were talking about perfection and limits at work. He told me that professionals don't have a problem knowing when they're overworking because they know how to work within boundaries. They know when to stop, when they've done enough. It made me think of an exhausted housewife and mother of two young boys who complained to me at an adult educa-

It is always possible to approach a goal by a detour.

THEODOR REIK

tion class that she works all the time and never finishes her work: she's cooking, decorating, gardening, cleaning, driving car pool, doing errands nonstop. "It's like mowing the lawn. Once I finish, then it rains, causing the grass to grow fast and it's time to mow it again." Laughing, I said, "You're alive, you're breathing. That grass will grow whether you mow it or not." We all have to work. But we don't have to overdo it. It's possible to approach our work with a balanced, wholesome awareness that we cannot be productive by overdoing it. By doing so, this woman may miss the best things in her life—her boys will be grown and out of the house before she knows what happened.

Another woman, Jane, confided in me that she feels guilty sitting still in her house. "At night I take a hot bath, have a cup of herbal tea, and go to sleep exhausted. I never have trouble sleeping because I'm always tired. But once the alarm goes off, I get up like a shot and go like a dynamo all day. I have to keep moving, doing something. The only time I sit is in the car, running errands." This type of schedule cannot be maintained. Two of her friends had to go get her and bring her to my talk because "she had work to do at home."

Jane is jittery. She seemed in a hurry as she waited to get a book autographed, even though her friends who were driving her home were behind her in line. Fascinated, I asked Jane to tell me about herself. "I'm a mother of three children, the wife of a doctor. We live in a large Victorian house. We entertain a lot. I keep myself pretty busy." Jane's friends laughed and said, "Alexandra, you should see her house. It is perfect." I exclaimed, "Oh no, Jane, you're not a perfectionist, are you?" She frowned, "I'm the worst. I go off the charts. I can't help myself." I got up from my chair and gave her a hug. I realized she really meant that she can't help herself.

A mother of two small children told me her story. She feels guilty because she works, so in order to compensate, she tries to be Super Mom when she's at home. Karen bakes bread and cookies. She shines the children's leather shoes. Everything a full-time paid nanny would do for the children in a day she condenses into a few hours, adding cooking, decorating, and laundry. She reads to the children before she's even read a letter from her sister. Karen insists the children eat at the dining room table with her and her husband, George, whose job it is to pour the water, juice, milk, and wine. He loves to compliment Karen on her gourmet meals, the table settings, the flowers. The only problem is that Karen is on the verge of depletion. She's using up her reserve emergency fuel. When there absolutely isn't anything you wouldn't do for your children, spouse, and house, the degree of sacrifice could be dangerous.

One is happy as a result of one's own efforts, once one knows the necessary ingredients of happiness: simple tastes, a certain degree of courage, self-denial to a point, love of work, and above all, a clear conscience.

GEORGE SAND

Each of us can learn how to stop overworking, and the sooner we do, the happier we'll be. Karen learned to serve food family style so she wouldn't have to act as a full-time waitress coming and going from the kitchen serving first and second helpings. Because she identified so strongly with her role as a mother and nurturer, she had to learn how to do some things for herself even when there was plenty she "should" be doing for the children, directly or indirectly. Nowadays, after the dinner dishes are done, Karen reads purely for her own pleasure, not doing any further housework. She is on the right track.

Whenever your habits are deeply ingrained, changing them will be difficult at first. Write down on a pad what needs to be done each day, as well as what needs to be done each week. For example, the laundry need not be washed every day. You do not want to turn your house into a Laundromat. Once a week is sufficient. Everyone will adapt to a weekly schedule, and this frees you up to do other things with your time. When you do laundry too often, you waste your energy. Settle on a day and discipline yourself not to backslide into doing it more often. Being too conscientious can be just as bad as being neglectful. Both are signs of being imbalanced.

Determine how many minutes you think it would be appropriate to iron. Then set a kitchen timer and when it goes off, unplug the iron and walk away, even if you have only ironed half a shirt. The other half can be done the next session.

Any form of compulsion indicates a lack of ability to stop. A compulsive eater finishes the cookies in the jar, the crackers in the box, the ice cream in the freezer, the peanut butter in the pantry cupboard. The overworked, like the overeaters, aren't aware of what's happening. They fall into a kind of trance where their behavior is on automatic pilot.

Any kind of overdoing needs reform. If you are constantly

No architecture can be truly noble which is not imperfect.

JOHN RUSKIN

And if you cannot work with love but only with distaste, it is better that you should leave your work.

KAHLIL GIBRAN

working on the house at the expense of doing anything for yourself, write a list of things *you* want to do and *do* several of them before you lift even a finger to a practical task. We all have to teach ourselves that our spouse and children will actually love us more as soon as we accept ourselves, identify our own needs, and take breaks from work.

Keep those lists handy. Check off what you do for yourself interspersed with your chores or routine work. Even when we love the work we're doing, we have to learn to ease up sometimes. Bake bread every other week instead of twice a week and treat yourself to store-bought loaves on the remaining days. Limit the number of hours or days you do housework as well as how much time you spend doing individual tasks. Plan one gourmet meal a week, perhaps on Saturday and Sunday, but don't attempt to have every meal a banquet.

Have a talk with your spouse and children. Let them know you love them and that you've decided to love yourself, too. Sit down together as a family and have regular visits where you do nothing with your hands except hold theirs.

There's no such thing as a self-made man. I've had much help and have found that if you are willing to work, many people are willing to help you.

O. WAYNE ROLLINS

We're all "constructively compulsive." We work too hard. Take more Zen time where you don't allow yourself to do anything, where you are present, in the flow of the moment, enjoying your family, your home, and yourself.

Overwork is as imbalanced and destructive to our happiness as disliking our work. When work becomes a burden in this way, it is no longer fun. Whatever we do we have to learn to sharpen our life skills, to be more professional about how we work and learn to mind our need for rest. Just because you cannot finish doing everything that's expected of you—by yourself or by others—doesn't mean you have to allow work to finish you.

Overworking in the hope that by doing so you will be perfect at what you do is, as we have seen, dangerous. Furthermore, perfection is neither possible nor necessary. In her book *How Would Confucius Ask for a Raise?* Carol Orsborn addresses the values of imperfection: "There is a tradition among Japanese gardeners, who, after their work is complete, scatter a handful of leaves so as to hold the inevitable turning point of the cycle of perfectionism at bay. Traditional American quilters, too, make sure there is a hidden imperfection in their handiwork."

Knowing when to stop working is indeed the art of the possible.

Making Your Situation Work for You

There are any number of reasons why we may be unhappy in our current work situation, but what's important is to do whatever we can to change that. This, too, is practicing the art of the possible. To the best of our ability, however gradual, we should try to move from an unhappy, draining, self-defeating work situation to something we cannot only live with, but find stimulating, absorbing, and challenging. Too many people have the fixed attitude that the job that earns them their living will never be enjoyable. They focus on everything negative about their work rather than on the positive fact that they have a paying job. There isn't a lot to be grateful for in *un*employment. Whenever we treat work as only a chore, it can only be a burden rather than a blessing.

One of the ultimate signs of success in life is to find joy in

If you are poor, live wisely. If you have riches, live wisely. It is not your station in life but your heart that brings blessings.

THE BUDDHA

the things you do every day. Part of what makes that happen is your engagement and involvement with your work, that extra effort you make to turn everything into a challenge. Whenever you pay special attention to what you do, when you care enough to do a little more, you elevate yourself both in your own eyes, and in the eyes of others. By shifting your attitude toward your job, even just 10 percent, you feel as though ten pounds of deadweight have been lifted from your shoulders. Complaining only makes matters worse. Whatever energy you send out, that's what you get back. If you're negative, you will get negative back. But if you're positive, well ... the sky's the limit. Doing the best you can, not seeking credit but enjoying the process and your efforts and seizing the opportunity to do a first-class job can turn many bad situations into potentially good ones.

Money may be the husk of many things but not the kernel. It brings you food but not appetite; medicine, but not health; acquaintances, but not friends; servants, but not loyalty: days of joy, but not peace or happiness.

HENRIK IBSEN

It's important to see how each individual task we perform feeds the well. Even when I'm vigorously cleaning my bedroom walls, I really get into the work. I do a section, stand back and smile at the brilliance. What a difference! I'm excited to do another section. It's a meditative, highly focused action. It's a little like Zen. Before I'm aware of the enormity of my accomplishment, I've completely cleaned all four walls. I take a hot steamy shower, put on a new red suit, and go off to meet a friend for lunch, terribly pleased and feeling physically wonderful. Work can lead to exhilaration.

Hard work brings satisfaction. When our eldest daughter, Alexandra, moved to Washington after graduating from college to begin a career as a journalist, she worked as a waitress at a restaurant in Union Station to supplement her tiny paycheck at *The Washington Post*. When she called to tell me about her job, I felt her exhilaration. "Mom, it really is fun. It's good for the soul." Not only did she meet many people who are now good friends but she found the work of serving others rewarding. There's no question that waiting on tables is hard work, but like everything else, the more involved you are, the more satisfaction you get.

In my village of Stonington, Connecticut, there is a young couple who do odd painting jobs together during the summer months. They're both art school students who want to become fine artists, and who earn money for school by painting picket fences and other things around the home. They chatter away, laugh at each other's jokes, talk to the neighbors who pass by, gets lots of sun and exercise, enjoy each other's companionship, earn enough money to pay for school, and feel really lucky to get work painting! They're so energetic and upbeat that everyone in our village wants to give them their business. They're in constant demand.

By focusing on what is possible, by putting all your effort into what you consider mundane tasks, you might get recognition and advance to a more responsible position. I had an intern who spent three months in Hong Kong while traveling around the world after college. After a couple of weeks, she and a friend were unable to find any work except doing filing for a large bank. The days were long and boring but they needed the money to keep traveling. Instead of going to work grumpy and reticent, they arrived on time and full of energy and did their jobs as well as they possibly could. Their attitude paid off. Soon they were noticed by one of the directors of the company and were given a highly responsible and interesting project working with banks around the world.

You can also make work more essential to your life and more

fulfilling by connecting with the people around you, and seeing your work as part of a bigger effort, perhaps connected to your community, or the greater goals of the company you work for.

Each of us brings our own personality to our work. In 1974, Emma Bolton was the receptionist at Doubleday, where my first book was published. I have vivid memories of our friendly visits, which have continued to this day by telephone and mail. She's still working even though she's past retirement age. Emma brings her jolly spirit to her job. She is not a lady behind a desk. Emma is a cheerleader encouraging the team. Doubleday published six of my books and even though they are no longer my publisher, Emma is the one who still forwards my reader mail to me. Emma's warm and welcoming manner made a difference to hundreds of authors who nervously awaited being called into an anticipated power meeting.

What would life be if we had no courage to attempt anything?

VINCENT VAN GOGH

No one who loves his or her work has an insignificant job. Emma made her job important by becoming a "link in the chain." If each one of us worked to be as strong and supportive of others as our humanity would allow us, we would indeed be able to strengthen not only our own feelings about work but about those for and with whom we work.

We all know what a difference it can make when we come into regular contact with cheerful, generous-spirited people. My day is always brightened when our United Parcel deliveryman, Fred, comes rolling down Water Street in his big, chocolate-brown truck. Fred always signals with a double thumbs-up; he's always there with a laugh, a smile, and a lively comment that lets you know he's glad to see you. And he delivers come rain, snow, or sleet. One time during Hurricane Bob, Fred stopped by, wearing high rubber boots and a slicker, just to see if Peter and I were OK. Everyone in our village looks forward to Fred's daily rounds, not for the packages, but for the joy and friendship he delivers.

And then there's Jean, at the post office, who takes pride in knowing something about every customer so that she can be personal, friendly and make business fun. She delights in showing you every new stamp. When there was a new flower series, Jean and I discussed the beautiful local gardens that we had just seen on a tour in our town. Whenever I do my errands, I feel grateful for this visit with Jean. Every time we encounter someone who cares about how others feel, everyone benefits. We feel connected, bound together in some special way, each doing our part.

Iron rusts from disuse, stagnant water loses its purity and in cold weather becomes frozen; even so does inaction sap the vigor of the mind.

Emma, Fred, and Jean practice the art of the possible. In doing the best they can under their own particular circumstances, they create joy for themselves and others. This in turn creates a sense of balance and contentment in a community.

Is it possible to do our work only with people we like? Rarely. Even Jean, Fred, and Emma encounter people throughout the day who may give them a hard time. If you're fortunate enough to have your own business, you can be somewhat selective about the people with whom you work. One of the most successful businesswomen I know deals only with people she trusts implicitly; people with whom she also likes to spend her time. "Hey, I work all the time. Even when I'm not physically at the office I'm on a business trip or thinking about a project. I might as well have fun." She's lucky indeed. But it's something we can all take an example from.

Even if you have to take a temporary job because your chosen work, as an artist or musician, for example, cannot pay the rent, a temporary job may be a means to an end while you are moving toward a greater goal. A young artist in our village had stars in his eyes recently as he told us about his day. During a recent heatwave when everyone was talking about how they were trying to keep cool, Ian was oblivious to the heat. Like Claude Monet, he was chasing after the sunlight and had painted several watercolors at the beach in Rhode Island before coming to work at a local restaurant. I asked him, "How was your day, Ian?" "Great, thanks," he replied. "Ever since I changed my shift from working at the restaurant during the day and trying to paint at night, I've become much happier. Now I can paint in the light, which is so inspiring. Before, it was dark. I was tired. I'd get discouraged. I'd come home from work beat, too tired to paint. Now, I'm full of energy and the productive day in the dazzling light actually brings me vitality while I work at the restaurant."

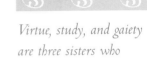

Virtue, study, and gaiety are three sisters who should not be separated.

VOLTAIRE

With some of the right adjustments, when you do what it is possible to do, you can set work in the proper perspective and achieve some balance, even when everything is not working in your favor.

Do What You Love and the Money Will Follow

Eleanor McMillen Brown's philosophy of work has been etched into my memory, guiding my career and life in inspiring ways ever since working with her. Mrs. Brown enjoyed herself enormously simply because she believed that if you do a good job, the money will follow. Even though she ran a large design firm, she was never focused on money. She didn't need to be, because

*Somehow his dream
is told: somehow he
publishes it with solemn
joy: sometimes with
pencil on canvas;
sometimes with chisel
on stone...*

EMERSON

she was too involved in designing and doing such a good job that the clients kept coming and paying. It was so inspiring to be associated with a firm that did the best quality work and, as a result, was successful financially. It all seemed so effortless, so civilized—the way it should be.

Mrs. Brown's advice was not only useful but practical; it is clearheaded thinking about the possibilities for a loving and rewarding working life. Though I have gone through several career shifts, I've strived for connection, flowing from one source of inspiration: my mother's flower garden. At the age of three I became fascinated with the sheer beauty, color, texture, and scent of flowers. When I was five I had my own garden club. We were industrious, as are all five-year-olds. We'd pick daffodils in April from an abandoned field above our property, an old onion farm at the top of a sleepy dead-end road with a view of Long Island Sound. We'd tie the bunches with colorful ribbons from Mother's wrapping closet, and off we'd go with baskets in hand to neighbors to sell our bouquets.

One old lady watched us from her living room window in anticipation of our arrival. She had delicious oatmeal cookies ready on a tray with ice-cold birch beer soda. Later that spring my mother told us, with a wink, that Mrs. Walton owned the field above our property. She was still delighted to purchase her own daffodils from us because she wasn't able at eighty-seven to climb the steep hill to her field anymore. We brought her own field's host of daffodils to her. When she moved to a retirement home in New York, my mother and I brought her a bunch of daffodils, tied in a familiar ribbon. This time I brought cookies and a soft drink to her bed tray. Her eyes sparkled with delight as the familiar daffodils brought back memories.

Rather than becoming a horticulturalist—my first-chosen "career," at the age of seven—I changed my mind to become an interior designer. That was the same year I planted my own garden at a summer farm in Laurens in upstate New York. My days were spent out in nature, which made me feel sorry for all the people who lived inside dreary houses. There is something depressing about curtains drawn for fear that the sun will fade the upholstery. Why couldn't those rooms be sparkling with dappling sunlight, clear colors, and energy from the outdoors, especially the garden?

From this childhood activity inspired by my mother's flower garden and my wish to create and tend my own, I slowly learned not only about what I needed to do with my life but some essential life lessons as well. Working in a garden taught me about both the order and uncertainty of life. Knowing that, gardeners learn patience.

Reflecting back over the fifty years since I had those first moments of awareness of what delighted me, I have come to believe that each of us has yearnings for things to move us from the very depths of ourselves. We are drawn to activities that stir our passions, which in turn may give our life meaning. Some of us discover this thrill in early childhood. But often those passions get buried as we mature. The burdens of making a living, raising and educating a family, as well as the pressures of fitting in and getting along in a complex society, often bury these intuitions.

I have been blessed in many ways that have helped lead me to the work I enjoy. My parents took me seriously at age seven, and arranged for a farmer to plow out a plot for my flower, fruit, and vegetable gardens. This meant a great deal to me. My first garden was

Creative work carries with it a form of intense love.

LIN YUTANG

I know that I have found fulfillment. I have an object in life, a task...a passion.

GEORGE SAND

one of those life-transforming experiences that I continue to draw joy from. Imagine being seven and excited about freshly tilled soil that was yours to plant and tend!

Staying focused on your talents, your skills, and your interests is what helps get you doing the right work for you. Once you have found that direction, everything, both important and insignificant, will gradually begin to feed your course. It starts a chain reaction and everything begins to fall into place. When you focus your energies, you create fresh possibilities; connections happen. You click into a new self-awareness and are better able to identify what you love to do. Whether you go to a career counselor to help you find out more about yourself or follow your known interests, the key is to own your destiny. It is yours alone. Others' expectations will never satisfy you. Once you find your "work," no one can keep you from it.

One man's story of such passion inspires me whenever I think about the often serendipitous ways in which we discover the work we love. For our twentieth wedding anniversary, Peter, Brooke, and I went to France. Before we left New York, a friend, knowing my love of Vincent van Gogh's work, made us promise to visit the van Gogh museum located in an inn where the painter died in Auvers-sur-Oise. From a brochure describing the museum we learned of its extraordinary origins. In 1985, a Flemish entrepreneur, Dominique Charles Janssens, while on his way home to Paris, had an automobile accident in Auvers. Janssens learned from the police report that the accident happened in front of something called the "van Gogh house." During his extended recuperation he decided to read the complete letters of Vincent van Gogh written to his brother, Theo. "When you read the letters, you find

*Art is long,
and Time is fleeting.*

HENRY WADSWORTH
LONGFELLOW

*Practice yourself, for
heaven's sake, in little
things; and thence
proceed to greater.*

EPICETUS

that there is a humanist hidden behind the maligned painter," Janssens told a Paris correspondent. "When you discover this, you discover another van Gogh." Intrigued by the coincidence of his accident taking place in front of the great master's home, Mr. Janssens learned that the building, which had become a café, was for sale. Feeling that destiny had sent him, he decided to buy the house and restore it as a cultural center "worthy of the humanist."

Occupation is essential.

VIRGINIA WOOLF

A year later, Mr. Janssens traded an important position in international business for the career of innkeeper. "Everyone thought I was crazy," he said, because he sold everything he had in order to buy the inn. Whether Mr. Janssens will ever be solvent again is not a major issue to him. "I did not buy a business, I bought the soul of a house that must be perpetuated," he concludes.

Our family adventure to Auvers revealed to us that soul. On a sparkling May Sunday, precisely 104 years after van Gogh arrived, he overwhelmed us with his presence. Even though our expectations were exceedingly high, our hearts were completely satisfied. I'm grateful that we ate our hearty lunch before we became enveloped in the powerful emotions of his personal space. "Accessible from the kitchen by a narrow wooden staircase, the room, spare and dark but for a swath of sun coming through a tiny skylight 'has a way of making each person who enters comfort himself,'" Janssens told the Paris reporter.

It is not from the benevolence of the butcher, the brewer, or the baker that we expect our dinner, but from their regard to their interests.

ADAM SMITH

After feeling the profound impact of this room, known as "the suicide room," which has been closed for a hundred years, we saw a slide presentation that brought tears to my eyes. Against the backdrop of this tiny, dingy, dank, bare room were this artist's vibrant, stunningly colorful paintings, making your heart thump, with a poignant voice-over reading touching letters to his brother, Theo.

Several months ago, Peter and I met with Dominique Janssens in New York. His passion is far-reaching. He told us that he never intellectualized his choice to buy this inn. It came to him, like a vision, and he had to follow that instinct. "I have no regrets . This was all meant to be. I made a choice, made out of love."

Anne Gordon has loved to draw since early childhood. After taking a ceramics class in art school in England, she took to the clay immediately. She'd found her life's work. Now, thirty-five years later, Anne is perhaps the greatest potter alive today, glazing her pieces in the eighteenth-century manner. Her birds, animals, fruits, vegetables, and flowers can sit next to ones two hundred years old and be compatible in quality and coloration. Her exhibitions around the world sell out immediately. Every piece is made by her hands and heart alone. She has no helpers in her studio and fires every piece in the kiln, around the clock in a downstairs studio. Anne loves what she does and is grateful that she is recognized and appreciated so she can also earn a living doing what she's found is her true passion.

It all takes doing—
and I do.

HENRY JAMES

Obviously, most of us are not in a position to pick up our stakes and buy our destiny, but we can be guided by love and devotion when we look for the work we will do in our lives.

The Chinese have a concept called *ch'i;* it is essential energy. By tapping into this, our own unique energy, we can find our destiny. By better understanding what releases and balances your *ch'i,* you will awaken even further to your talents as well as your life course.

How Stephanie and Walter Achieved Excellence by Following Their Passion

Through a combination of talent, enterprise, and sheer will you can achieve not only excellence, but can create a working environment that works for you. Stephanie and Walter recently opened a restaurant in our village after becoming increasingly disenchanted with the deterioration of New York City. For ten years Walter had been a versatile chef at a large popular restaurant. Then he escaped the city for our picturesque fishing village and opened his small Water Street Cafe. A local paper, *The New London Day*, awarded the restaurant four stars. We were finally able to get a dinner reservation, and we were greeted that evening by Walter's wife, Stephanie. This attractive lady, who manages the restaurant, was also waiting on tables that night, like an angel, clad in one of the aprons she had designed and made for the whole staff. Stephanie described with elation to Peter and me the fun she'd had mowing their lawn that morning for four hours. "I lost all track of time. It is *so* beautiful having a big lawn." Her right thumb had a bandage wrapped around it concealing a large blister. Stephanie works all the time and loves it. She's so appreciative to be in the fresh air in such a sweet village, away from the craziness, intensity, and traffic of New York.

Walter and Stephanie found a way to fulfill their needs. And their attitude and joy made the project work. The space they took over was small with only enough room for nine tables and a minimal-efficiency

To myself I seem to have been only like a boy playing on the seashore, and diverting myself in now and then finding a smoother pebble or a prettier shell than ordinary, whilst the great ocean of truth lay all undiscovered before me.

SIR ISAAC NEWTON

There is no ecstasy like that of creation.

LOUIS AUCHINCLOSS

kitchen. Nonetheless, Walter and Stephanie's cafe is packed every night. Walter conjures manna from heaven. He combines his own herbs to create amazingly exotic, subtle flavors. People make reservations far in advance and come from great distances to celebrate an evening of delicious food in the cozy atmosphere they have created. There's a strong sense of pride among the local regulars, grateful to have another superb restaurant in the village. With intense work and flair, Walter and Stephanie created a wonderful treat for others.

Stephanie's daughter Danielle, age sixteen, also waits on tables, and Walter's daughter Shannah, eleven, serves food in this heartening and friendly place. One evening during an extended heat wave, while the restaurant was exploding with patrons, the fan belt broke. We were sweating buckets. Next to our table an architect from Providence valiantly got up on a chair, reached up to the ceiling fans, and turned the switch up to high. We felt instant relief. Everyone spontaneously clapped and cheered. Some diners had left the restaurant to go outside to get air between courses,

Industry, thrift, and self-control are not sought because they create wealth, but because they create character.

CALVIN COOLIDGE

yet no one complained. Everyone was caught up in the devotion of this family working together, achieving excellence through enterprise, talent, and sheer will.

Stephanie and Walter have won all our hearts. When parents in the village have a child getting married, they throw a private party at the restaurant. Or they'll ask Walter to cook the food at the reception. You anticipate having a good time at their cafe and leave with a sense that you're blessed. In a cynical age, how refreshing it is to combine excellence, experience, family dynamics, and genuine warmth and love. You return home feeling touched by caring friends.

We all respond well to the rewards of hard work. Beyond being refreshing, work brings hope. When a project is yours, you can take pleasure as well as pride in your accomplishments and enjoy the fruits of your labors.

The only way to receive abundantly is to give abundantly.

PETER MEGARGEE
BROWN

3

Time

for

Play

If you are losing your leisure, look out;
you may be losing your soul.

—LOGAN PEARSALL SMITH

Living Takes Time

Everyday life is rich in miracles. A joyous, balanced life that partakes of these small miracles is always available to us, no matter what our circumstances. On any given day there are mountains to climb, sunsets to watch, streets to wander, children to play with, art to enoble us, and people to love. Life offers us an endless supply of wonderful experiences of beauty, pleasure, enlightenment, tranquillity, and exhilaration. But we can only receive these gifts when we take the time to play with our possibilities.

Play is the exultation of the possible.

MARTIN BUBER

Time for play? Who has time for play? We all do. Despite the avalanche of demands that confront us every day, there are remarkable opportunities to feel the joy of being alive. Our problems will be there when we return; but, after play, we will be refreshed and reinvigorated, and therefore better equipped to take on the challenge of daily life.

Playtime is the time we let go, ease up on the burdens, obligations, deadlines, and pressures that drive us forward. Play can entail anything that allows you to lose yourself in the moment, anything that is intrinsically pleasurable. Psychologist and author Mihaly Csikszentmihalyi calls this state of absorption "flow." You can be in flow when taking a walk down Main Street or a hike across the desert, when you climb a mountain or become transfixed by the birds and the trees, when you take photographs, dance, plant in your garden, lose yourself in an antique store, or just pick up your feet and fall into a great book. When we are focused on this dimension of play, a world of possibilities for pleasure opens to us. Everything can be better. Our ability to taste, touch, see, smell, and hear becomes enhanced. Life is a joy.

In fact, when we lose our desire to play, we know something is going terribly wrong with our lives. Years ago, I went to visit a friend who was recovering from a nervous breakdown. I asked her how it felt—when did she know she was in trouble? "Sandie, I lost interest in everything. You know how much I love to play tennis. You know how much I love my boys and William. You can't imagine how it feels not to have fun. I lost interest in opening my eyes in the morning. Even my addiction to chocolate vanished. I stopped reading. I was dead. When I no longer had fun playing, I knew I needed help."

Too often we refuse to let go of work and choose instead to deprive ourselves of a real break. We think that by willing ourselves to do more, we will find stability, security, and satisfaction. But without rest, our lives become a tightrope walk; we're constantly trying to stay on top of work, family, health, and chores without losing our balance. As any athlete will tell you, unless you know how to relax your muscles and rest them, they will tighten up, even snap, and every movement will cause pain. Simply willing ourselves across the tightropes of life will not keep us up for long. Many problems can only be solved after a long rest or by backing off. Taking breaks for fun or relaxation prevents us from becoming stiff and stuck, so that when we return to our tasks, we are more flexible, less strained, and better able to balance ourselves—or at least it gives us a chance to set a cushion down should we fall.

It was with this same understanding of life's processes that

> *He who acknowledges the imperfectness of his instrument, and makes allowance for it in discussing his observations, is in a much better position for gaining truth than if he claimed his instrument to be infallible.*
>
> WILLIAM JAMES

*A song is no song
unless the circumstance
is free and fine.*

EMERSON

my friend Eleanor McMillen Brown used to say,
"Living takes time." Now that I've lived a little
longer I think I know what she meant: We cannot
force or rush our work to completion. If you're trying to write a book you will not be successful by
doggedly writing twenty-four hours a day. The ideas
and insights you need take time; sometimes you have
to wait for those to come, or you might need to stimulate your imagination and enhance your creativity by seeing a
movie, looking at a painting, or just stretching your body by taking a walk. Likewise, living takes time because life is a creative
process. We need to alternate industriousness with spontaneity.
A full life is not made of work alone.

Play feels timeless. That's why when we play we say we are
taking "time off." Indeed, when we play we feel absorbed and
lost in it. We forget about time, chronological time, that is.
Though we may not be aware of it there are two dimensions of
time. In *A Circle of Quiet,* the writer Madeleine L'Engle writes of
the ancient Greeks' wisdom about these two different senses of
time:

> The Greeks had two words for time: *chronos* and *kairos.*
> Kairos is not measurable, it is ontological. . . .In kairos we
> are, we are fully in isness. . .fully, wholly, positively. Kairos
> can sometimes enter, penetrate, break through chronos:
> the child at play, the painter at his easel, the saint at
> prayer, friends around the dinner table, a mother reaching
> out her arms for her newborn baby, are in kairos.

Chronos, or chronological time, is separate from kairos.
Chronological time, by its very nature, does not allow us to get
lost in a moment. It is exact, while kairos is expansive. In

chronological time we are always aware that time is moving on. As a society we have become so chronos-oriented, so overly scheduled, that we are constantly trying to condense more and more into less and less time. But the truth is that whenever we race against the clock—whenever we become too time-bound—the clock always wins. If this other dimension of time were not available to us, we would feel frustrated and defeated by life all the time. After all, there's never enough time to get everything done in time.

The great man is he who does not lose his child's heart.

MENCIUS

When we play, we take off our watches.

Play gives us the freedom we sorely need. When we're not slaves to our schedule, we have greater possibilities to play and achieve flow. In play we connect directly with whatever we're doing. Temporarily, we lose our self-consciousness, our insecurities, our doubts, our fears, our anxieties, and our anger. Why? Because when we are engaged in something we passionately enjoy, we lose ourselves in the experience. I love to leave my desk and walk out to the point of the peninsula in our village to sit on some sun-warmed rocks. I lose myself in the sky, the water, the boats, the wind, and the waves. My mind wanders and I feel the power and beauty of life. This fills me with a sense of life's infinite possibility.

One ought, every day at least, to hear a little song, read a good poem, see a fine picture, and, if it were possible, to speak a few reasonable words.

JOHANN WOLFGANG
VON GOETHE

I also love to watch children play, to listen carefully to their banter and see them transform themselves from monster to maiden in the whim of the moment. They get inside experience completely. During play we can all open up to the mysteries and wonders of our lives, taking great leaps into the unknown and the undiscovered in ourselves. In play we connect directly with what we're doing. When we run along the beach or wander through a museum, we live inside those moments with a certain abandon. When we stop trying to be efficient we become absorbed in what is.

There is no pleasure in having nothing to do; the fun is in having lots to do and not doing it.

MARY WILSON LITTLE

Playtime, this time out of time, is critical to maintaining balance in our lives. It allows our souls to breathe. Without it we suffocate in *shoulds* and *musts* and *do-it-nows* and *make-it-betters*. Play, by its very nature, releases us from such judgments. No one can tell you how to play or that your sense of pleasure is wrong or not good enough. Through play you discover what delights you, what moves you, and what you really enjoy. You get back in touch with yourself.

This is real living and indeed it does take time. The secret to a balanced life is to build play into your schedule every day of the year.

Value Yourself Enough to Play

It is an all-too-sad fact of life that many of us neglect our most precious opportunities for joy because we are convinced that other things are more important. I have a friend whose boss brags that she's "never had a day off." Some people think they're only living when they're working. Still others think they can only have fun after they've done all of their work, or collapsed from doing too much of it: "If I can just finish cleaning the house after I get home from work, I can take some time off on the weekend." These "workaholics," people who believe that their value in life is measured by the amount of work they do, are living under a terrible delusion. The workaholic believes that if she does enough, or even too much, everything will then be taken care of. But there are no pipes that never spring another leak, and there is no end to difficult bosses or clients. We'd have to be under some powerful spell indeed not to see that there will always be problems.

Living life well is about knowing that you can try to get everything done, but anticipating that you will fail. When you know that, you will definitely take time out for fun. The trick is in how you juggle your many demands into a fulfilling life. Working on a business report while running a laundry, bathing a child, and filing your income taxes is definitely not the formula for a stable, happy life. If play and relaxation are not in the building blocks that support your life, the whole edifice will come tumbling down on you.

Exaggerated and abstract expectations of productivity create a terrible imbalance in our lives. Not only free time but time that is devoted to our own particular pleasure tells us who we are. Knowing what we like to do is essential to a healthy, rich life. It's impossible to work continuously at all the facets of your life with enthusiasm without taking some real breaks. Play is not a throwaway indulgence. Everything worth doing is worth doing well. To live your life well, your life must be worth living as well as it can within your abilities and opportunities. I owe a great deal of the quality of my life, my sense of happiness and calm, to my avid interest in play. I love how play makes me feel. It holds equal weight to my work.

Mingle some brief folly with your wisdom.

HORACE

When you overwork you are operating from a mistaken understanding of why you work so hard. Thinking that doing more will make you a more valuable person, you pile on more and more. But in the end, you produce less and less. And you feel empty. Your desire to overachieve doesn't necessarily come from wanting more for yourself, but rather from expecting less for yourself. People who overwork do so because they believe they are unworthy of being just themselves. If you take the time to notice how you are feeling, you will see that there are other things you'd rather do with your time. When you say *no* to overwork, you say *yes* to yourself.

A man must keep a little back shop where he can be himself without reserve. In solitude alone can he know true freedom.

MICHEL DE MONTAIGNE

Perhaps one of the most important lessons an overworked, perfectionistic person can learn is to walk away from her work and back to herself. That is not to say that our work doesn't express anything of our self and our passions. It does. But when work needs to be done to the exclusion of everything else, it is no longer being done out of the desire for self-fulfillment, but rather to crowd the self out. I've learned to walk away from work because both my work and play are so important to me. I wouldn't want either to suffer. I've learned that the essential secret to a balanced life is to ease off and walk away on a regular basis. In my travels across the country talking to women, young and old, I am struck by how many of us feel unworthy of taking time away from work and from helping others in order to do pleasurable things for ourselves. Young mothers, especially those who work, have enormous difficulty incorporating carefree fun into their brutal schedules. Perhaps it's because they haven't been at it long enough to know that fun time is only ignored at great expense. Often, it is difficult to recognize this. But what better means to learn the spirit of play than from a child?

Many of us cannot stop ourselves from taking care of business when we see that something needs doing. For many women it's a reflex. In our orientation to care for others—husbands, children, and parents—we may neglect ourselves and therefore take on more and more projects instead of taking time to rest and play. Modern life doesn't help us to regard this as an imbalance. All the ease and speed given to us by advanced technology seems not only to have failed to make life easier, it's made us even more busy with things to do. When faxes can be received day or night, and the office can be taken with you to a restaurant or the beach via cellular phone, even the old reliable times for play and relaxation are gradually being weaned away from us. Modern life has become even more crowded and therefore more difficult in the end.

For we that live to please must please to live.

SAMUEL JOHNSON

Once we believe that by our very humanity we deserve the time to play, we will discover that there is no end to our opportunities for pleasure. By caring for yourself, loving yourself as much as you love anyone else, and wishing for yourself what you wish for others, your life will grow with possibility. And the demands of no one, not children, spouses, bosses, parents, friends, or your community—or even yourself—will be able to take play time away from you for very long.

Walking Away from Work Toward Play

On a recent afternoon, a friend passed though our village and, seeing the flag up at our house, she assumed we were in. When no one answered the door, she was surprised and walked around to the back to take a peek in the windows to see if we were there. When she saw the dishes in the sink, she assumed I was home. No one leaves a house with dirty dishes. I do!

As far as I'm concerned, we've allowed too many *shoulds* to get in the way of living. The bed doesn't have to be made before you listen to a piece of music or write a poem. The dishes don't have to be done before you take a walk or a dance class. The dust will still be there after you play, and so will the dishes. When you play first, you do your work or your chores later with a sense of greater pleasure and satisfaction. As Dr. Eric Butterworth, a spiritual philosopher, says, "Do your best and leave the rest."

Sometimes the people you work for, whether they're at home or at your job, have a hard time letting you ease up or say no to their constant demands. Resist. We can't expect others always to understand what we need for ourselves. As a mother you may have to make an arrangement with your husband to take care of the children, perhaps for certain set times of the day, so you can have time to go out with friends or see a show. As an employee you will have to make sure your boss does not intimidate you out of taking regular breaks or biannual vacations. Even doctors aren't on call all the time. There have to be times when you give yourself unqualified permission to relax and the freedom to walk away. Make a deliberate effort to build playtime into your life—even if you have to race out of the office or drop what you're doing to get to where you can play.

The only true time which a man can properly call his own, is that which he has all to himself; the rest, though in some sense he may be said to live it, is other people's time, not his.

CHARLES LAMB

When I was working as a decorator at a large design firm I had a client who not only had an apartment in New York but also had inherited a large colonial house in Massachusetts. Whenever he wanted something from me, I jumped. There wasn't anything I wouldn't do to meet his needs. I saw to it that he got number-one service every workday for over a year. One August weekend, I had the pleasure of sailing off the Maine coast with a group of friends. I returned to Southport, Connecticut, on Sunday night, refreshed, relaxed, and exhilarated from the trip. Over dinner that night my then-mother-in-law informed me that she had received an irate phone call from a client of mine on Friday evening, at nine-thirty! She repeated the conversation to me verbatim: "I want to speak with

Sandie. It's urgent. This is Mr. Patterson." Connie told him I couldn't be reached until Sunday night. "What do you mean?" he shouted. "Give me the telephone number where she is. I need to speak to her immediately." Then Connie gently told him that she couldn't help him; that I was on a thirty-seven-foot sailboat off the coast of Maine and there was no way I could be reached.

I love this story because anytime I feel guilty or bad that I might not be available enough for others, it reminds me that "enough" for others can be much too much for me. And when I stay focused on getting my time to drift or play, I know that what I give myself and others is neither too much nor too little; it is balanced and enough.

I know now that if I work too hard, I become critical of myself and lose the flow of vital energy I need to do creative work. Whenever I feel too pressured, when I'm caught short of time because of unrealistic deadlines, and when everyone around me becomes anxious as well because of this, my productivity and effectiveness are sorely compromised. And when everyone around me starts looking grim from overwork, it makes me nervous. That's the time to stop. Instinctively, I know it's time to play. Do I finish my work before I goof off? Absolutely not!

Why clean your house on a sunny day when you can be outside instead?

As happy a man as any in the world, for the whole world seems to smile upon me.

SAMUEL PEPYS

If A equals success, then the formula is A=X+Y+Z. Where X is work, Y is play, and Z is keeping your mouth shut.

ALBERT EINSTEIN

Creativity and Play

The best place to really witness the creative power of play is in the playground. Psychologist and teacher Erik Erikson believed adults could learn more from children. "You see a child play and it is so close to seeing an artist paint, for in play a child says things without uttering a word. You can see how he solves his problems. You can also see what's wrong. Young children, especially, have enormous creativity, and whatever's in them rises to the surface in free play."

Children work out tremendously difficult problems in their play. They do so with creativity and innovation. Just watch how a child dares to make a two-foot stack of wooden blocks retain its shaky balance, or how a living room becomes a landscape of mountains and caves with the simple use of a sheet and a couple of chairs, and you'll know a lot about what can be done if one plays with abandon. Children enjoy the free use of their imaginations and the freedom to do only what pleases them to meet the challenge of learning. And we all know that when learning is fun, kids learn more.

Play is serious business. Play stimulates the imagination and keeps our minds flexible. Play releases powerful hormones and endorphins and increases our sense of pleasure. Play challenges us to solve problems, which keeps us focused. Play allows us to fantasize about having other identities, which opens us to the experience of others. Play allows us to test our limits by seeing how far we can climb or how playful we can be. Play allows us to experiment and

In leisure there is only the present.

DR. JAY B. ROHRLICH

Rest is not idleness, and to lie sometimes on the grass under the trees on a summer's day, listening to the murmur of the water, or watching the clouds float across the sky, is by no means a waste of time.

SIR J. LUBBOCK

therefore enables us to stretch the limits of the possible. All childlike behavior encourages joy, creativity, and innovation.

The true touchstone of wit is the impromptu.

MOLIÈRE

Perhaps the most productive players in the adult world are artists. I've long appreciated the tremendous capacity for playfulness in the creativity exemplified by painters and sculptors. You can see the power of play in their work. Artists are inordinately curious about the world. They love to try things out, to experiment with different ways of capturing experience. They are not only interested in creating something new, but they are interested in the discovery process that's involved in that creation. They change the colors on their palettes to create a whole new world. They play with different mediums, optical illusions, and our preconceptions about the world. They try for the sake of trying when they explore where a little idea will take them. This is play at its best.

From the radiant beauty of Claude Monet's gardens to the passion for form and color in Henri Matisse's rooms and the ladies in them, artists celebrate what is and what they see in ways that stretch all of our capacities for understanding the world and our experience of it. Children's paintings are a revelation of how problems are solved through creativity. Children paint what they see and sense. By doing so, they communicate something authentic and true, though not necessarily realistic, about the world. If a child isn't certain how an arm grows out of a body or how a tree is set into the ground, his attempts to answer that question in his drawing tells us everything we need to know about how we make judgments, how we solve the problem of representing a form even when we don't know how to do it exactly. Pablo Picasso, perhaps the most prolific twentieth-century artist, was the living incarnation of creativity.

Her ways are ways of pleasantness, and all her paths are peace.

PROVERBS 3:17

He created in every way, shape, and form he could—using whatever material and surface he could mold into sculptures and ceramics, paint into pictures or objects reconstructed into collages. Looking over a cross section of Picasso's output is to experience the creative spirit in action. Without play, there would be no Picasso.

Leisure is a mental and spiritual attitude. . . an attitude of contemplative "celebration" which draws its vitality from affirmation.

JOSEF PIEPER

We're not all artists, but we can all be creative through play. We can live with the alertness, sensitivity, and openness that characterize the artistic approach to life to find new ways of experiencing life for ourselves.

The work of artists teaches us so many things about the sustaining role of creativity throughout our lives. For many older artists, that playful, free spirit helps them to find solutions to the problems of their changing abilities. When Matisse became ill later in life and found it difficult to stand up and paint, he lay in bed and created brilliant cutouts and collages of paper. Georgia O'Keeffe, who continued making art until she was ninety-eight years old, began to work with sculpture and ceramics instead of paint on canvas when her vision began to fail. We can learn from this as well.

We must give ourselves permission to play as extravagantly as artists and children do. In fact, if we don't, we risk depleting ourselves and even burning out. People who understand this know how to introduce elements of play into their own work. Whenever you succeed at integrating work and play, you've created an opportunity for euphoria. This is the art of the possible. Everyone has the potential to benefit from this concept. Even for those of us whose work requires precision and analytical thinking, using the power of free play can help us crack a stubborn problem. Much research and experimentation has been devoted to the role of play breaks, relaxation, and spontaneity in the workplace. Time and again these studies find that the most productive workplaces are the ones that respect the need for play. How many times have you heard stories about the great achievers in history whose problems were solved when they were taking a break? Albert Einstein discovered the key to his ideas about relativity while relaxing in his hammock, not while sweating over a book. Albert Schweitzer once explained that the secret to his success and happiness was his appreciation for fantasy. And Thomas Edison was known to have napped while stretching across his desk any number of times during the day.

We cannot live by intellect, nor hard work, alone. We need to let loose, not only to hunker down. Play releases tension, opens blocked thinking, boosts energy, and balances our immune systems. Many of us get the answers to our questions not when we're struggling but rather while we're in the shower, listening to music, or even as we're falling asleep. Some believe that if you ask yourself a question before you go to bed, when you wake up you will have your answer. Play releases your unconscious—the other half of your brain—to work while you do not.

As an experiment, log in how many hours you work per week. Include everything: how much time you spend at home working for your family, at the office, store, or factory, and volunteering for your community. After adding the hours of work, figure out how many hours you use for play. Recording these numbers will help you to understand better why you feel so exhausted or stressed. Or, if you've struck the right balance, you'll see the reason why you feel creative and so terrific.

. . .leisure and a quiet mind.

HENRY DAVID THOREAU

The wisdom of a learned man cometh by opportunity of leisure; and he that hath little business shall become wise.

ECCLESIASTICUS

Making Your Own Fun

Peter and I were at Kennedy Airport in New York waiting to board a flight to Paris last February when we saw a Yale classmate of his and his wife. At an airport a safe question is, "Where are you going?" When Bill asked us where we were going, Peter smiled and answered, "Paris." Bill asked, "What are you going to do there?" Peter answered with an added chuckle, "Nothing." Silence. The conversation immediately closed on the whole thought of "doing nothing" in Paris. "We're going on a safari," classmate Bill said. Well, now there was an opportunity to have a real discussion. Africa is full of color, action, natural beauty, adventure.

It is all a frame of mind, this enjoyment of living.

LIN YUTANG

Their flight was earlier than ours so we wished them a great journey. Peter kissed me once we were alone. When you tell someone you're going somewhere "to do nothing," why does it have a threatening or dull, sad ring? The only thing we had to do was physically plump ourselves on French soil and "be." Paris has a splendid way of taking care of you, no matter what your interests are, whatever your mood or circumstances. Having a crowded schedule would destroy the opportunity to let the city cast her spell. Generously, the art, the beauty, the light, the architecture, the grandeur, the elegance, the food and wine, the people-watching fill your experience with all one could ever hope to experience. When you leave to return to your real world, you reflect poignantly on the pleasure of having had the freedom to do what the spirit moves you to do, at the spur of the day, letting the city pour her riches upon you from dawn to dusk.

Modern life is too busy. I derive enormous happiness from

settling into whatever I'm doing, not having a tight agenda or cramped time constraint where I feel trapped. Rushing is like living with a chronic headache. What's ironic is that the more we're in a hurry, the less we enjoy the process and, because we're out of balance, the less productive we are, so even our future goals suffer. Fast is never gracious, no matter how you rationalize the expediency. Quick fixes are usually short-lived. If it takes you ten years to gain ten pounds, losing it in two weeks won't mean a great deal ten years later.

Rushing, being anxious, feeling frantic and frustrated over details is an escape from reality because you can work yourself up to such a state that you feel self-righteous about your self-imposed deadlines. Who says we need to condense time? Like breathing, there is a rhythm, a flow, a naturalness about our existence that will lead us quite well if we don't interfere.

Modern society is not to blame. We are. When we speed ourselves up, we trip and fall. Driving ourselves to do more in less time, to be more efficient rather than make time for the sweet things in life, has a price. We shouldn't be willing to pay for the toll of this acceleration, away from a well-balanced, good life.

The key is learning to walk away from unfinished work. You don't find time to play amid the busy-ness of work. You take time, you *make* time, by removing yourself from your work environment.

Some of us have unwittingly agreed to work all the time. Between faxes, portable phones, and business hours all day, every day of the week, there's little delay between one activity and another. We've gotten used to crowding in everything that we can. As a result, many people

I often went fishing in Maine. I like strawberries and cream, but I have found that, much to my dismay, fish prefer worms. So when I go fishing, I do not think about baiting my hook with strawberries and cream. Rather, I look for big, juicy grasshoppers and worms.

DALE CARNEGIE,
TOLD TO ME BY
MY BROTHER POWELL

have lost the ability to know what to do with their unstructured time. Some may fill leisure time with passive mind- and spirit-numbing activities like watching television. Television creates the illusion that we are being stimulated by life, when in reality it dulls our senses and leaves us feeling tired. Sadly, some people, when faced with a bright beautiful day, will grow despondent over what to do. They know they should be doing something but don't know what that something is. Having been driven by the demands of cleaning, working, or caring for others all week, they have no idea how to turn their attention away from others back to themselves. What would engage me? What would give me pleasure?

Curiosity is delight.

WALTER CHARLETON

The opportunities for play and pleasure are everywhere. On a recent Sunday afternoon while sitting on the porch reading, I heard someone call my name. When I looked up, I saw that it was our minister and friend, Mark Robinson, waving to me as he whizzed by on Rollerblades shouting, "I'm having my Zen time." Zen time is the name we in our family give to relaxation, play, or solitary time. It is the time when we do things for the pure joy of it, when we make room for spontaneity and for the delight it brings us. It could be a long vacation or a ten-minute break. Zen time reminds us how to get back in touch with ourselves and what makes us feel good. When we take Zen time the simplest things—a conversation with a friend or a warm summer breeze—will give us tremendous pleasure.

Things don't give us anything except what we bring to the enjoyment of them.

LIN YUTANG

Because we learn so much about what delights us when we play, we become more in tune with these pleasures. Peter, for example, loves to observe the world around him when he takes his Zen time. He goes on long, leisurely walks where he mentally records everything that captures his imagination. He examines old architecture, listens to the sounds of the village, studies the changing colors of nature, and most of all is moved by all the relationships between things and people. When Peter walks around the shops in our village, he's always on the lookout for interesting crafts, antiques, or something to beautify our house. When the spirit moves him, he enjoys polishing the brass or silver or even hanging a picture. When he's near a museum, he enjoys learning about history and art. The spirit of letting go is not to do nothing but rather to be free of the things you don't do for your own pleasure or benefit.

Once you have learned not to be driven to overwork all the time, you will discover, as Peter has, that there are many things that you like to do. No matter how tired you are from a week of work, you will find that you always have energy for fun. We all naturally gravitate to anything that enhances our sense of well-being. Paying positive attention to ourselves makes us feel good. The biggest obstacle toward that may be you. There is infinite potential for turning simple things into stimulating challenges. Carving out a special time when you can lose yourself in some simple but absorbing activity is the key.

During periods of relaxation after concentrated intellectual activity, the intuitive mind seems to take over and can produce the sudden clarifying insights which give so much joy and delight.

FRITJOF CAPRA

Maybe the spirit will move you to hang a set of dessert plates on the dining room wall, or clear out a drawer in your kitchen, putting a favorite place mat on the bottom as a colorful drawer liner. There are as many different kinds of things to do when we play as there are types of work. It's all in your selection, matching up what will bring you pleasure with the activity. Sitting at the kitchen table or at your desk and writing a child a really long, intimate letter is a gift you give yourself. When we ease up on the obligations of life, allowing ourselves to appreciate what we have from a wider perspective, we find that every action we take, when it springs genuinely from our heart, is a loving one.

While we're replenishing ourselves, we're also doing things that often bring pleasure to others, too. A dad might invite his son to go for a swim or boat ride or to go fishing. Your spouse might want to go on a bike ride and invite you to come along. A mother could have an urge to look at family pictures and put them into a scrapbook.

How good is man's life, the mere living! how fit to employ / All the heart and the soul and the senses forever in joy!

ROBERT BROWNING

One of my favorite pastimes is to putter. There are times when I don't want to commit myself to any one activity but I'm in the mood to move around and do whatever I find delight in at the moment. I touch certain objects. I might hold a paperweight up to the light. When we are free, our senses are more receptive. We become more aware, more open.

When you work at home or at a home office, taking time off is particularly important. You don't have the change from a business atmosphere to home, so you have to create it where you are. My Zen room is where I work. Often I get up from my desk with everything all set up, I turn out the overhead light, and go downstairs. Simply by changing locations, I'm able to switch gears from work to play. Have a specific place where you work so you can come and go without having your work interrupted. Once you're in the flow, you can walk away from your work and, miraculously, when you're playing, it continues to take shape.

Discipline goes both ways. Some people find it difficult to set limits to their work when they have a home office, turning their house into a work trap. This is a shame. In our New York apartment, Peter enjoys working at his desk by the windows in our living room. Even without leaving this attractive place, he can walk away from his desk, sit on a chair by the fire or on the sofa and read a book or a magazine for pleasure. The desk is the work spot. When he's not there, he's free to play.

When Peter and I are both working from home, we discuss our intentions ahead of time. It is possible he will want to work in the afternoon and I'll want to play. We work out a schedule so both of us feel free to do what's right at the time without disturbing the other person's concentration. Several summers ago, he was working on a lawsuit that required his full attention for several months, while each day, I enjoyed finishing my work before lunch so my afternoons were free to play. Because he has a real office, with fax, Xerox machine, telephone, and all his files, he was free to occupy his time without inconveniencing me. We'd meet for lunch and again for an iced-tea break in the garden, which was something we both looked forward to daily.

When you're able to arrive at a healthy balance between work and play at home, you'll find, as Peter and I have, that the atmosphere is so warm and friendly. Both activities are enriched because you're in your own personal, meaningful space, set up to nurture and support you throughout your day and evenings. I do all my work from home and find this is also my favorite place to play. When we're able to move effortlessly from work to play and back again to work, like flipping the same coin, we discover the endlessly rich possibilities for constructive, productive work laced with interludes of spontaneous, lighthearted play. This rhythm is intoxicatingly luring. I find it hard to beat.

Play refreshes and heals us. So whether you pick up knitting needles, paint your ceiling sky blue, play in the sandbox with a

Variety is the soul of pleasure.

APHRA BEHN

Age does not make us childish, as they say. It only finds us true children still.

JOHANN WOLFGANG VON GOETHE

Pleasure is produced by the union of excitement and affection.

BALZAC

one-year-old (yours or anybody's), go for a drive in the country, play tennis, ride horses, play the piano, or write a story, you will feel reborn.

But do what's right for you. No one else's fun can be better than your own. When I was in the south of France teaching classes at an international conference, there were lots of planned activities for fun. But all Peter and I wanted to do was to see friends, wander around Provence on our own, go to cafés, people-watch, take pictures, and linger over a delicious lunch while sipping the region's wines and soaking in the local color. That may not do it for you. *You* don't get full by watching *me* eat. The only criterion for fun is that you be fully engaged in what you're doing for your own sake.

There is also an art to play. As with everything worth doing, playing takes practice, and sometimes skill. By all means, start out by letting yourself go. Let yourself try anything: write, paint, dance, run, read, draw, hike, watch birds, make pottery, do yoga exercises. Don't be afraid of not being good enough. Just do it. And then, after you've had some practice, you'll feel even greater pleasure. The more you play, the more skilled you get, and the more you enjoy playing. The more tennis I played, the more fun I had because I learned to do it well.

The honest man takes pains, and then enjoys pleasures.

BENJAMIN FRANKLIN

Make a deliberate effort to build playtime into your life. Even if you have to race out of work, or drop what you're doing to get to where you can play, do it. It's is a great relief. It's like a balm of soothing lotion massaged into your back after an exhausting day.

Enjoy the Playful Spirit of Summer All Year Round

The novelist Edith Wharton once said that the two sweetest words in the world are "summer afternoon." Not only do the warm, sunny days of summer weather feel like a blessing but somehow everything in the summer seems touched with grace. In summer we plan to have fun. Even our clothes turn more playful and colorful in summer. We wear silly hats, take picnics in the park, camp at the lake, and stroll in the evening. We play more sports, spending more time in natural light, and become more playful and happy all-around. Longer days and brighter light renew our sense of well-being. Everything is better in the summer. In summer we let ourselves play.

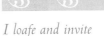

I loafe and invite my soul.

WALT WHITMAN

I first learned about the epiphanies of summer twenty years ago when our family spent July and August on the beach in Marbella, Spain. It was there that it became brilliantly clear to me how central play is to our lives. We spent that whole summer on the beach which was, naturally, the most popular place of activity for our children. But soon enough we were all drawn into its spell. We hardly ever wore clothes. We felt utterly free.

We don't have to lose that playful spirit of summer when winter comes. Though we may pack away the picnic basket and take in the lawn chairs, we needn't shut down our spirits. Learn from summer how to play. One of the joys of summer is light. When we lose light, we lack energy. Something as simple as increasing the wattage of your lights from sixty watts to a hundred or a hundred and fifty can make you feel better in the dark winter days. Indoor living need not demand rigid formality.

*Productive activity
is characterized by
the rhythmic change
of activity and repose.
Productive work, love
and thought are possible
only if a person can be,
when necessary, quiet
and alone with himself.
To be able to listen to
oneself is a prerequisite
for the ability to listen
to others; to be at home
with oneself is the
necessary condition for
relating oneself to others.*

ERICH FROMM

Make the kitchen the heart of your home. In winter, we can spend more time in the kitchen, gathered around the enveloping warmth of what is my favorite room in the house. Dim the lights and dine in the kitchen. Never mind what your parents may say. "No man is a hypocrite in his pleasures," wrote Dr. Samuel Johnson. I'm sure that if my mother were alive she'd love to sit at our old farm table in the kitchen and have a real visit.

How can we make the atmosphere where we live more playful? Try to use some of the same happy colors of summer in your home in the winter. Perhaps you can use your beach towels in your bathroom. Why not? In the summer, we don't care when we drag in the sand from the beach; we don't worry about perspiration after an exhilarating tennis game. We ease up on our cleanliness standards. There is a direct relationship between the amount of fun you're having and the amount of dirt you make. While I may write about the pleasures of having colorful, attractive dust cloths, it doesn't mean you have to live dust-free. I get nervous when I'm in a house that's too clean. I'm not suggesting that we all become slobs, but I am suggesting we all relax our standards so we have more time and freedom to play in winter, too.

A Play-filled Day

We each have our memories of great days. I'd like to share a little story about one day that gave me what I want out of the spirit of play. Recently Peter and I were out in California on a book-promotion tour. As a very special event, a group of our friends planned to have tea and a visit after a book signing. Marilyn flew in from St. Louis, and my next-door-neighbor Mary Ellen and her darling five-year-old daughter, Darcy, from Connecticut, were visiting friends, so they all came. Our dear friends Devin and Claire came, as did Carmen, Jamie, Sally, and Lorna. There was such a feeling of warmth at the bookstore that we began inviting more and more people to join us at our hotel.

This was such a joyful day. Darcy, Marilyn, and I went to a great flower store where Darcy picked one flower for each person, matching up a flower for each personality. The strange white one looking like a feather duster was selected for Claire. Before we paid for it, we were swishing it around tickling each other with its long, spaghettilike petals. We bought a scented candle; we went to a candy store and let Darcy help pick out some candy; then off we went to our own celebration. Later, in the room, we watched the magnificent sun setting over the Pacific as the waves, crystal clear and green, pounded on the rocks of the cove below us. A celebration that began at one o'clock at a bookstore, my seventh visit there, broke up around eight o'clock in the evening when most everyone left the tea party. Then Carmen, Marilyn, Peter, and I went to a restaurant for a delicious dinner celebrating my birthday.

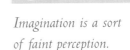

Imagination is a sort of faint perception.

ARISTOTLE

The gathering grew into a serendipitous, spontaneously happy event—unrepeatable, amazing, and memorable. Not one person there resisted the happening. In a Zen consciousness, being fully present to this magical moment that lasted seven-plus hours was the main ingredient to happiness. We had a happening and it made us all happy. This happening, so uncontrived and innocent, is happiness, and I suppose the result of the exhilaration and the resilience that are born of play.

PART TWO

Remaining Centered

4

Health

and

Healing

To keep the body in good health is a duty....
Otherwise we shall not be able to keep our mind
strong and clear.

—THE BUDDHA

Health Is a State of Mind

What is health? A person in excellent health is functioning at an optimum. Everything—body, mind, and spirit—is working well and in balance. According to his theory of health, Japanese healer Hakuyu says, "When the five activities—obtaining nourishment, [having] movement, perception, study, and realization of the purpose of life—are out of harmony, then the structure of the body goes wrong."

Having good health does not mean you will never get sick. We all have to grapple with colds, flus, broken limbs, and pain of one kind or another. Some of us have chronic problems such as ulcers, arthritis, and back pain. And many of us will have to confront much more serious illnesses. Our health will be tested. It's impossible to go through life without suffering both physically and emotionally. But it's absolutely possible to live without bringing unnecessary suffering on ourselves.

Nature balances mind, body, and spirit as co-creators of our personal reality.

DEEPAK CHOPRA

There is a world of difference in how we feel when we resist and deny our condition and when we approach illness with the understanding that we have possibilities for happiness beyond our illness; that we can always take some form of action to help ourselves. When we approach illness this way, we are in balance, and that contributes to our healing. A balanced perspective means, paradoxically, that when we can accept that we will not always be well, good health becomes more possible. Denying our limitations and expecting ourselves to be in perfect health undermines us and makes us sicker; insisting on the impossible always puts a strain on us. The real secret of good health is that we will feel most healthy when we respect and accept our limitations. Health is not only a physical state; it is also a state of mind.

I consider myself an extremely healthy person, yet I've had my fair share of severe medical problems. I've spent time in hospitals having surgery. While it would be great indeed to be guaranteed that we will never need an operation or have to take strong medications, we know that in life things are always breaking down and being put back together again. Just as you become solidly situated in your job, your boss is replaced by a difficult person. You feel yourself in peak condition in the summer, but winter comes and you inevitably fall ill with the flu. When we accept our limitations and know that things will go wrong—and we cannot always prevent it—we are more able to cope with problems when they arise.

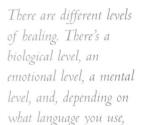

There are different levels of healing. There's a biological level, an emotional level, a mental level, and, depending on what language you use, a spiritual level.

DR. MICHAEL LERNER

Being healthy means knowing we are whole as we are; we are not missing anything. In the words of the Greek Stoic philosopher Epictetus: "He is a man of sense who does not grieve for what he has not, but rejoices in what he has." We have within ourselves all that we need to cope with the losses and enjoy the rewards of a full life. When this is our basis for health, though we may be physically ill, our mind and spirit will make us well again.

Even when we pay close attention to our health and well-being there will always be conditions—physical illness, emotional pain, mental confusion—that are beyond our control. The more we resist these facts of our lives, the more shaky and anxious we will feel. "Healthy" is feeling whole even when something breaks. I used to be a headstrong "can do" person.

Health is not just an absence of illness, it is a way of living.

BILL MOYERS

However, when I permanently damaged my back from playing so much tennis over thirty-five years, I learned about doing only what I can. It's no longer possible for me to hold a racket and a few balls in my right hand without risking injury. After much grappling with this loss—which to me was a great one because I played tennis all the time—I knew that I was unwilling to take the risk of exerting myself on the tennis court when several doctors had advised me never to play again. Certain risks are simply not worth taking. Good health is about making wise compromises. And with this I learned a lesson about the power of acceptance. By learning to let go of what I could no longer do, I gained the ability to strive for what is possible. As soon as I accepted my condition, I felt whole within myself. I was confident that I would open a new door after this one closed. While I will never play tennis again, my acute back pain is behind me. I exercise and live pain-free every day.

The only test of a soul's salvation is its inward happiness.

LIN YUTANG

A friend in weakening health lamented to me, "As soon as I grew up, I crumbled. I can hardly get out of bed in the morning. I'm full of aches and I creak around in chronic pain. What a waste to finally feel grown up and to have no zest for living." This is a woman who just turned sixty. I meet so many people who hold on to their resentment for what they cannot do—or no longer have—instead of discovering what they can. We heal ourselves and stay well by our desire to get on with our life.

Good health emerges, I believe, when we are able to accept ourselves as we are and not overreact to what we are not. Good health is having patience and not judging yourself and others harshly. Good health is doing things in moderation and not always trying to outdo yourself. Good health is admitting that

you have neither ultimate control nor all the answers.
Good health is knowing how to laugh at your problems and knowing when to cry. Good health is knowing how to balance your losses with gains.

With all this said, good health is not easy to
achieve. If it were, more people would be well. Good
health comes to us through a process of taking care
of ourselves on every level of our being: body, mind, and spirit.
And like everything important in life, good health requires conscious, deliberate maintenance. The process by which we maintain our good health is by exercising our healing abilities. There
are countless ways. The well-known American-Buddhist teacher
and psychologist Jack Kornfield illuminates the healing way in
his interpretations of the ancient wisdom of Buddhism in
Buddha's Little Instruction Book.

*One learns more from
adversity than when
times are easy.*

DAVID ROCKEFELLER

- If your compassion does not include yourself, it is
  incomplete.
- Life is so hard, how can we be anything but kind?
- Everything in moderation, including moderation.
- There is only one time when it is essential to be awake.
  That time is now.
- Stay centered, do not overstretch. Extend from your center,
  return to your center.

The healing process takes many different paths.
What's critical, though, is taking the path toward a
positive, active role in everything that happens in your
life. By holding yourself accountable for how you feel,
in some fundamental, existential way, you will have
some measure of good health even when you are sick.
There is always something you can do to improve

*Into each life some rain
must fall,/ Some days
must be dark and
dreary.*

HENRY WADSWORTH
LONGFELLOW

your condition or situation. We have all heard the many amazing stories of self-generated healing, people who recover from some cancers and other "incurable" illnesses even when the odds were against them, because they did something about their condition rather than let themselves be undone by it. While we should be careful not to judge ourselves if we cannot turn a chronic or terminal condition around by our own efforts, we can learn a powerful lesson from such situations. And that lesson is that we have an impressive power over our own lives, the power to make ourselves well. I'm not talking about the power of positive thinking here, but of the power we gain when we accept ourselves, take responsibility for our health, and seek out peace in our lives. When our lives are balanced in these ways, we know that though we may be thrown from a horse, the important thing is knowing whether it's time to get back on or time to walk away. When you focus on getting well instead of expecting to be in perfect health, healing is always possible.

There is truth in sadness as in happiness.

JOHN BOWEN COBURN

Healing the Body

I like to walk about amidst the beautiful things that adorn the world.

GEORGE SANTAYANA

Being accountable for your health and taking action on your own behalf are essential to the healing process. Many people, however, take this too far and turn their healing into an obsession. If, in trying to stay physically healthy, you spend hour upon hour at the gym on any given day and become consumed with taking megadoses of vitamins or if you go on an extreme diet to stay slim and deny your body the balanced nutrition that it needs, you will not heal; you will hurt yourself instead. The effort to maintain peak condition and perfect health can itself become a sickness if we require it to maintain the illusion of total control over our lives. Running, working out, or pressing weights to develop well-defined muscles may give you a feeling of control in your ability to shape your body, but it will not prevent your body from needing rest or from growing old and changing. There is no such thing as a perfect body that always yields to our will. We have to respect our own individual capacities for physical

We never know how high we are / Till we are called to rise.

EMILY DICKINSON

exertion; every body is different. It's not fair to expect your body to be able to do strenuous exercise if you have a bad back, or if you're prone to getting flushed and dizzy when you work out. It's good to push yourself, but when you push too far, you inevitably hurt yourself. Though it's certainly exhilarating and admirable to stretch yourself a little beyond what you have done before, overreaching may contribute to a fall. Moderation is the key to good health and balance.

For several years, I had a private trainer come to my apartment early in the morning two or three times a week in hopes of strengthening my back. However, being the competitive person I am, I kept wanting to increase the intensity of the workouts. I ended up using heavy weights as I jived around the hall to fast music. After class one morning, my back was killing me. Even after a long hot soak in the tub, I was still in agony. Later that morning, I tried to move a potted plant and ended up in acute pain. On another occasion, my back pulled

Health is not a condition of matter, but of mind.

MARY BAKER EDDY

out just by standing up, a result of overexerting myself while exercising earlier in the day.

We can also learn to balance ourselves by taking time off. When I returned from Chicago after my brother Powell died, I knew I couldn't focus on my work. I canceled all my appointments and didn't even attempt to think clearly about anything work-related. Later that morning, I spontaneously began to try on the dresses in my closet, some of which I hadn't worn in years. Soon I found myself giving an impromptu fashion show to an audience of Peter and my two assistants. We had so much fun judging each outfit and pinning the dresses to new lengths. For the first time in days, I felt a sense of relief. I needed to take a carefree day for myself, one without extreme sorrow or the responsibilities of work.

Everything has its wonders, even darkness and silence, and I learn, whatever state I may be in, therein to be content.

HELEN KELLER

Exercise, dancing, participating in a sport, and physical exertion of any kind are great contributors to a healthy state of mind and body. It's been well documented that chemicals, called endorphins, which give us a sense of well-being and joy, are released in our bodies when we exercise or engage in continuous movement of any kind. Watch anyone who has just jogged around a park or bicycled for twenty miles and you'll see someone glowing with delight and alive to his senses. I get this sense of exhilaration, this wholeness, often when I clean the kitchen floor or wax our wood floors. Not only do I get the floors clean and gleaming, but I feel enormous satisfaction from doing the work myself. It makes me feel radiant physically. You get energy from exerting energy.

The Healing Power of Walking

Walking is just about the best exercise I can do. Even in my darkest moments of pain, a walk has always been a way to heal myself. The cardiologist Dudley White once said that there isn't much that can't be cured with a five-mile walk. Walking improves circulation and allows our spirits to breathe. I always feel vitality infusing my whole existence when I take a walk. I feel loose, open, and happy. We are sweetened by our walks. Walking is not only enjoyable and healthful—it's fun.

Walking gives you time and space to relieve tension. Recently I complimented a bookseller on how gracious she was. She said that this was the result of an important lesson taught to her by her father, a village physician who lived to the age of ninety-two. During a period of confusion in her life her father made her promise always to wait twenty-four hours before registering a complaint with anyone. That way, she could release tension and keep her problems in perspective. Walking can serve that purpose as well. Taking a walk away from an anxious situation, whether at home or at the office, helps you clear your head and sort things out. A good walk brings you back to yourself. When I walk by myself, I'm able to pay attention silently to inner feelings.

I take every possible opportunity to walk. Often while I'm entertaining friends, I'll jump up and offer to get something, maybe some chocolate chip cookies on a tea tray, just to be able to stretch my legs and walk. I love walking through cities seeing beautiful architecture. I love walking through my town and saying hello to friends. Taking a walk when you hear bad news or have been cooped up with someone sick is extremely therapeutic. Having a standing walk date with a friend is delightful and intimate. Some people like to talk things through with others when they're having difficulty, but often, I'd rather walk alone. Walking gives me the solitude to work things out for myself. I often take a small pocket notebook

There is no education like adversity.

WALT DISNEY

In the depth of winter, I finally learned that within me there lay an invincible summer.

ALBERT CAMUS

with me and write down ideas and images that float to mind while I'm walking. This helps me keep a healthy state of mind.

Our Mind Affects Our Body, Too

Taking care of our physical body is not enough for radiant good health. Our thoughts have a tremendous effect on our bodies and our emotional health, too. Each thought, emotion, and mood releases chemicals from the brain that in turn affect our body and our spirit. In recent years there have been many books, articles, and television shows that explore this powerful mind/body connection. Doctors like Bernie S. Siegel, the author of *Love, Medicine, and Miracles*; scientists and healers like Joan Borysenko, the author of *Minding the Body, Mending the Mind*; and thinkers like writer and television producer Bill Moyers have revealed powerful evidence of the mind's ability to heal the body. The stories they share about the lives of people who have overcome terminal illnesses, people who had been given six months to live but who went on to live for years, or people who have slowed the deterioration process, are an inspiration to us all.

Learn to let go. That is the key to happiness.

THE BUDDHA

Feelings are chemical. When you get scared, for example, your fear sends a chemical message from your brain to your body telling it to sweat, tremble, flee, or feel faint. Persistent negative thoughts affect the immune system perhaps because they tax the system too much and weaken it so that we become vulnerable to illness. Often chronically depressed people become chronically ill with colds, ulcers, viruses, pain, and a host of unexplainable physical complaints. Few of us can be perpetually cheerful or optimistic;

that's not where the problem lies. The problem comes from a pattern of attitudes, of constantly thinking and judging yourself weak, sick, helpless, fearful, and incompetent, or always feeling angry and irritated. Illness can also come from demanding too much of yourself, insisting that you always be perfect, happy, and on top of everything. These attitudes can put a strain on your system. Mind-sets determine whether we approach life with a sunny disposition or a bleak one, and that in turn affects our health. Henry David Thoreau seemed to have understood this when he wrote: "Measure your health by your sympathy with morning and spring."

Birds sing after a storm; why shouldn't people feel as free to delight in whatever remains to them?

ROSE KENNEDY

Our capacity to adapt to life's challenges is key to our health and well-being. We become vulnerable when we fail to meet our problems in a balanced way. According to Dr. Richard Totman, author of *Mind, Stress, and Health*, whenever we become stuck—which he calls a "blocked action"—an overwhelming sense of hopelessness takes over. When we are unable to initiate and carry through activities that express our aliveness, it causes stress. This stress then upsets our chemical balance, weakening the immune system. It is not how much life stress we have, but how we manage it that determines our health.

This is not to suggest that there is no room for negative feelings in our lives. Certainly, that is not the case. Expressing anger, pain, or hurt is good. It's when you keep those feelings locked inside or overindulge in them that they can become destructive to your well-being.

The illnesses of perfectionists have a powerful mind-body connection. Perfectionism compromises health. Because of their excessive and unrealistic demands of themselves, perfectionists put greater stress on their bodies, sending powerfully destructive signals from their mind throughout their body. The perfectionist cannot tolerate the body's natural limitations. When she is happily working, achieving her goals, she is fine. But should illness or incapacity come, the perfectionist is without resources and is ill-prepared. Many perfectionists experience burnout, which leaves them with unforgettable emotional exhaustion.

Know how sublime a thing it is / To suffer and be strong.

HENRY WADSWORTH
LONGFELLOW

Perfectionists become anxious about the need to succeed always. This, combined with the loss of control during illness, knocks them off balance. The accumulation of physical and emotional strain releases hormones that can lower immunity to illness. Whenever we fail to acknowledge our limitations, no matter how we persevere, we become stressed and lose our ability to cope. The mind-body communication for the perfectionist is a powerful contributor to both physical and emotional illness.

I was told a story by a friend about a beautiful young newlywed who, on her honeymoon, began to think of hundreds of reasons why she couldn't move into the house her husband had just bought, because it wasn't "perfect." Less than a month after her wedding celebration, this young woman, barefoot, in nightshirt and underpants, checked herself into a hospital desperate for help.

Perfectionists, knowing that the mind can increase susceptibility to illness, may also judge themselves failures whenever they get sick. This is a terrible distortion. Sometimes we're just in the wrong place at the wrong time. When I got strep throat a few years ago, I was miserable. Two or three days later, Peter caught it. When I asked our doctor what we should have done to prevent this he said, "You should have stayed away from each other."

Perhaps nowhere is the communication between mind and

body more dramatically in evidence than in the placebo effect. A placebo is a medication that does not actually treat the disorder for which it is prescribed but improves the condition of a sick person because he believes that it will. I'm fascinated by the whole idea of a placebo. I've read that one third of all placebos improve the patient's condition, and though they don't work on every illness, placebos can improve a host of problems from anxiety to migraines, coughs, and arthritis. What this shows is that our ability to believe we are being cured helps us to recover.

Though our environment and our heredity are critical factors in our vulnerability to cancer and other less life-threatening diseases, the things we think and feel can either contribute to or lessen our chances of becoming ill. Scientists today can describe more clearly the powerful communication between mind and body and how it affects our health and the healing process. Hope, patience, and perseverance seem to have a lot to do with our ability to get well.

For me, it's not the prospect of a cure that reassures me that I will return to good health, but my determination to face my problems squarely without losing myself in them. I always try to look at the larger picture. I try to explore my possibilities within whatever illness I have. I tend not to complain. My doctors wish I'd fill them in on some of my symptoms earlier than I do, but I always innocently assume that I can regain my health myself. Though of course this is not always so, for myself nor for others, I find that, in most cases, whatever sickness I have (and they've been minor; that is, no devastating illnesses) in time, heals itself. Obviously, there are many illnesses and injuries that will not simply heal themselves. We often need medical

Do you imagine the universe is agitated? Go into the desert at night and look at the stars. This practice should answer the question.

LAO-TZU

help. But in those areas where there is room for attitude to make a difference—as seems to be the case for pain, for example—we can contribute greatly to our healing.

Illness as Teacher

"A wise man should consider that health is the greatest of human blessings, and learn how by his own thought to derive benefit from his illnesses." These words of Hippocrates, physician of ancient Greece, seem to have anticipated what we are only now learning about the link between attitude and health, and about what illness can teach us about our lives, both physically and spiritually.

As in the physical world, so in the spiritual world, pain does not last forever.

KATHERINE MANSFIELD

When we get sick we learn who we are both as individuals and as human beings. Illness can make us more self-aware. When we are sick we face ourself intimately. Among other things, we recognize our limitations, our unique boundaries. We see that when we push too far, we break down. In illness we are confronted with our broken self, which reminds us that all human beings have limited control over life. Therefore, knowing how to cope with that broken self is the key to our strength in living. When we accept our own individual strengths and weaknesses, eventually, we always know how to put ourselves back together again. A good life is not one in which we never get sick. A good life is determined by how well we live in spite of infirmity.

When we have health problems, we have to readjust our priorities. When I was told that I had to lie on my back indefinitely until my back healed, I had to take a good look at my obligations. I was in the midst of doing a lot of decorating at the time, which meant I had to send my assistant in my place to supervise various jobs. I'll never forget the morning she came to me with a kitchen-cabinet door so I could approve the paint color. I was suddenly struck by the realization that despite my temporary disability, everything was running smoothly. Not only did I learn to trust others during my recovery; I also discovered the wisdom of delegating. If I hadn't injured my back, I never would have found out just how capable my assistant was.

Wounds which we inflict on ourselves are the most difficult to heal.

THEODOR REIK

Disease has something to teach us, something to say. Sometimes, though not always, our illnesses are indications that we have gone off course, that we have lost our way.

The day that my brother Powell died, I took a walk by myself in the snowfall, oblivious to the coldness of the air and the moisture seeping through my shoes. I hadn't eaten properly or slept well while he was in the hospital preparing for his open-heart surgery, so my resistance was low. I was unbearably sad and confused. Friends told me to take care of myself but I simply couldn't. As a result of my emotional pain and fatigue, I came down with a dreadful, debilitating cold.

A physical or a psychological illness can also tell us we are not getting the love from others or the attention we need from ourselves. When we collapse from running ourselves down, rushing to do too many things, our body and spirit may be asking for nurturing attention. Sometimes, when we find ourselves in bed with a fever, our helplessness forces us to receive warmth and care from others, care that we all need. In illness we learn that it is not only OK to depend on others, but that such relationships can be healing for all involved.

Even if you are a strong person, that doesn't mean there aren't times when you need sympathy. When you are ill, for whatever reason, it is an appropriate time for people to show their love for you in tender ways. A few days after my brother's funeral, I was coughing and sneezing, my nose was red and sore. My daughter Brooke immediately took charge. She brought me cold medication, yellow tulips, herbal tea, and sat on my bed and tenderly became my care giver. Her love and affection were just what I needed. She has a magic way of knowing just what to do. I felt loved and blessed to have her there to help me through a difficult time.

Before my brother Powell became ill, Peter, Brooke, and I planned a six-day excursion to our favorite city, Paris. With the grief and anguish surrounding my brother's death, we asked Alexandra to take time off work to join us because we felt that life is short and we all really needed to be together. One week before we were scheduled to leave, we received a phone call that Peter's brother had died of a heart attack at his home in Naples, Florida. The news was shocking and sudden. Peter's tragedy made this family escape even more important to us. The mere fact that we were together as a family gave each of us strength to cope with our loss and pain. Sometimes just being together is all that is necessary to help in the healing process of a loved one.

It is by forgiving that one is forgiven.

MOTHER TERESA

We also learn from illness the power and importance of our feelings for other people. As night follows day, Peter caught the flu and cold I had come down with while in Chicago tending to my brother. Peter was terribly sick, and I felt bad that he had became so ill; every time I'd hear his deep cough I just knew how weak he felt. I hated seeing him suffer, and I worried that perhaps he had pneumonia. His illness made me acutely aware of how much I love him and just how important he is to me.

An illness also can be a warning that you are not living your own life. A friend was on a vacation in Florida when she was rushed to the hospital with a bleeding ulcer. After an operation and a period of recuperation, she confronted the source of her physical ailment: the emotional pain of a marriage that was tearing her apart. Having faced the turmoil in her soul that led to her ulcer, she is now separated from her husband and feels she is on the road to healing.

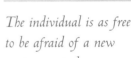

The individual is as free to be afraid of a new venture as to be eager for it; free to bear the consequences of his mistakes as well as of his achievements.

DR. CARL ROGERS

On another level, illness can be seen as an opportunity to grow. There is much we can learn from the stories of people who face serious illness with acceptance and resolve. These self-healers, it seems to me, see their illness as an opportunity, a challenge to discover things about themselves and about life that they can use in a positive way. Some people even describe their illness as a gift that enables them to see aspects of life they would not otherwise have appreciated. I can understand this because my mother told me in a letter before she died that it was worth her getting cancer and dying to be able to have the opportunity to be close to me. A friend once asked me if my mother appreciated me. I knew she did, deep inside, but she had difficulty expressing her love and affection. But when she knew she didn't have long to live, she broke down her guard and expressed her feelings openly to me.

In contrast, many people cannot accept their illnesses. They refuse to acknowledge what is and consider themselves weak and totally responsible for their condition, or they feel victimized and tyrannized by it. They become afraid of their own minds and bodies. When we refuse to accept our limitations we may become obsessed with every ache and pain, and with everything that goes wrong, becoming hypochondriacs. When you can only see illness as a sign that your life is imperfect and therefore intolerable, you miss the opportunity to deepen your understanding about the full dimension of life.

For people who can face up to the challenge that illness brings, life can become richer; they can discover new strengths in themselves. For those who are open to what their illness can teach them, life becomes more vivid and precious. Facing your illness enables you to discover how to live in the here and now and take every moment as it comes. When this happens, time itself seems to slow down and expand. When you live within yourself today, you feel no pressure to run away from yourself toward an ever-unreachable tomorrow. Living in the here and now is indeed a gift.

Often, when I have been sick or have faced the pain of loss, I feel a strong urge to celebrate life. The day I was discharged from New York Hospital after minor surgery, Peter and I went straight to Harry Cipriani, a favorite Italian restaurant in Manhattan. We had a delicious lunch of grilled shrimp, sautéed leaf spinach, a mâche salad, and a glass of chardonnay. Every bite tasted wonderful. I could feel all my blessings in this simple affirmation of life. Isn't it a joy to know we can participate in life every day? We can smell the warm summer air, love others, eat tasty foods, walk along the beach, wake up to a new day. All too often we do not appreciate the life we have and constantly think about what's around the next corner, never alive and happy with where we are now. We are so often planning ahead for a tomorrow that never becomes a today.

For those who see illness as an opportunity rather than a shutting off from the world, illness helps them make a new connection to it. It can give depth and greater meaning to life. I once watched a television interview with a writer who had been told by his doc-

The purest and most thoughtful minds are those which love color the most.

JOHN RUSKIN

No one can make you feel inferior without your consent.

ELEANOR ROOSEVELT

tor that he had only three months to live. I was mesmerized by this man. He was positively glowing with appreciation for living and respect for what was to come. He was extraordinary in his fearlessness. He remarked that when you know you are sick and dying and look out your window and see a tree as you've never seen it before and hear the sounds of children playing as an exquisite delight—you discover the real meaning of being alive to life.

In Lauren Bacall's memoir she remembers the final day of John Wayne's life. He was acting in his last movie, and the producers and staff on the set knew it. One morning a cameraman arrived at the studio in a joyful mood, declaring to everyone, "Isn't this a beautiful day!" John Wayne stood for a moment, shook his head, and replied in his measured way, "Every day you wake up is a beautiful day."

In periods of recovery, whether from an illness, an addiction, or an operation, we are forced to confront ourselves and this gives us a new opportunity to act. It has been well documented that after a tragedy or illness, we learn to make major life changes. Illness has much to teach us about the very process of life and its basic truths.

Grant that I may not so much seek to be consoled as to console; to be understood as to understand; to be loved as to love. For it is in giving that we receive; it is in pardoning that we are pardoned; and it is in dying that we are born to eternal life.

ST. FRANCIS OF ASSISI

Our Health Affects Others

When we're in good health, we're in the flow of life. We have the freedom to give of ourselves. Everything seems possible. We're grounded, but we feel as though we're soaring. We are active and energetic. In these peak moments we forget our handicaps and

enter into activities that engage us, body and soul. The people around us benefit from our positive energy. But whether we feel sick or well, those around us are affected by how we deal with our problems.

When I was twenty-five years old and pregnant with Alexandra, the doctor's orders were to stay trim and gain no more than fifteen pounds. I went on a strict diet, avoiding butter and oil, and eating the blandest food. I ate cantaloupe filled with cottage cheese for lunch. Everywhere I went I carried a miniature peppermill with five different kinds of pepper corns to spice up my bland diet. I put so much pepper on my food that my eyes teared and my nose and sinuses were always clear. I felt nervous every time I went to the doctor's office to be weighed by his nurse, who was terribly stern. As a result of this fat-free diet, when Alexandra was born, her skin was dry. She also developed a taste for peppery, spicy food later in life. She puts Tabasco sauce on absolutely everything that goes in her mouth, which led friends to nickname her "Pepper." But she is so bouncy and buoyant, so full of life that the name becomes her. Did she develop this craving for pepper in utero as I sprinkled it constantly on my food? Is her dry skin condition the result of my diet?

Interestingly, I had the opportunity to watch my second child, Brooke, develop through a very different approach during my pregnancy with her. My original gynecologist had retired, so I found a new doctor who believed it was good to gain more weight than I had with Alexandra. As a result, I relaxed and enjoyed olive oil and vinegar on my salads. I even ate some fried foods. And I indulged in my favorite food of all—which I had been deprived of for my nine months carrying Alexandra—avocado. Today, Brooke is not only addicted to avocado, but she is also a very calm person. And she was born with the softest skin, as though she'd used my favorite treatment product, Molinard's Creme 24, a blend of sweet almond oil and lemon. I'm convinced that these differences in my diet had the consequent effect on each of my daughters' skin, temperament, and tastes.

Certainly some of these characteristics don't come out of the blue. I always marvel at how powerfully we affect each other. What I ate and drank, and my predispositions during pregnancy seem to have influenced my daughters' lives in the womb. But our attitudes to life and problems also affect each other on a daily basis. Not only do we set an example for others, but we can also be of help or hindrance to others in their own illness or in times of loss.

I gain strength from loved ones when I am going through a difficult time, and am comforted to know that I am able to be a comfort to others in their times of need. Sometimes just listening is all that is needed of us. Shortly after Powell died, I called John Coburn, whose presence at the other end of the telephone seemed miraculous. His voice, his attention, his support, meant so much to me in my dark despair. I felt his strength and understanding as I admitted how broken I felt. Our closeness allowed me to regain my balance when I felt so alone.

Someone else's life can often be the example you need to bring you through a tough passage. I've been fortunate to connect with readers I've never met face-to-face who look toward me in times of need. I'll never forget receiving a telephone call from a reader after her second child was born. The call came from the neonatal-care unit of a California hospital. This woman's first child had been born prematurely and, after months of struggles to try to keep Megan alive,

The patient sitting before me brings with him or her not only chemistry, but also family, relationships, emotions, and character...a whole person...ideally we would deal with all of these aspects— the balance of a person's life.

DR. DAVID EISENBERG

How seldom do we behold tranquility!

EMERSON

she died. When Carrie's second baby was born, he weighed only one pound, eight ounces. She called me in despair. I felt grateful I was there to receive her call, to listen to her fears, and to love her during her most painful hours.

Who do you look up to as a good example in your life? Who would you turn to as a help in a crucial time for you, due to illness or the loss of a loved one?

Coping with Illness by Concentrating on Healing

What's significant about not being 100-percent healthy is not how sick you are but how well you cope. Everyone has their own way of coping with illness and suffering. My preferred style is to try not to dwell on it. I've never been cured of pain or sickness by getting more absorbed in it. When I do dwell on it, I don't enjoy my own company. When I pity myself, I only end up making myself more pitiful. I have faced many illnesses and tragedies in my life and I know from painful experience how ter-

In a dark time, the eye begins to see.

THEODORE ROETHKE

ribly hard life can be. But I also know from experience that you can face life's greatest challenges. When my brother , Richard, committed suicide, I was devastated beyond words. Many people said I had every reason to be clinically depressed. I wasn't.

One of the toughest realities in life is not knowing what to expect. Certainly the most painful aspect of my older brother, Powell's, surgery when he had a massive stroke was not knowing whether he would live or die. When my younger brother, Richard, jumped out of a four-story building in New Haven, Connecticut, he became immediately brain dead. Although he was being kept alive by the artificial means of a respirator, everything was concrete and definitive. My brother was dead. In many ways, it is easier to face this reality than to have him miserable in a mental institution, heavily medicated, unable to be himself or to function among family, friends, or in society.

I actually felt relief for Richard when he died. For years and years he couldn't snap out of his misery and was, quite literally, beside himself. My brother chose to serve in the Vietnam War, and the trauma of his experience never left him. Because he was an amateur photographer, the United States government decided to station him here, where he was assigned to take photographs of the dead soldiers who were returned from the war zone. In his agony and desperation, he took LSD and never was himself again. I did what I could for my brother, including trying to persuade the doctors, with the help of our minister, to remove the respirator. I feel strongly that when there is something concrete you can do to help someone, do it. When you can do no more, you let go.

Endurance is only the beginning. There must be acceptance and the knowledge that sorrow fully accepted brings its own gifts.

PEARL S. BUCK

I was expected to mourn Richard's death. This grieving we experience when someone close to us dies is normal and necessary in order to begin the healing process. The fact that I was there, two hours after my brother's suicide attempt, to do whatever I could, helped me to face reality and cope with a horrible situation. There is a universe of difference between the sadness you feel when you face a terrible fact of life and the depression you fall into when you cannot deal with the facts of your own life.

We heal ourselves and stay well by our desire to get on with our lives, by being involved with others, by doing interesting projects. When we participate in life we can experience a turn-about. Rather than dwell on our illness or brokenness we can focus on being well, not only physically but emotionally and spiritually, too. By taking better care of ourselves this way, we take care of not just the disease, but of our whole being.

It is possible that we can learn to influence the balance that maintains health in relation to the outside world.

DR. ROBERT ADER

To achieve this focus on what is possible, we must focus on our options when we are faced with illness or pain. We know that all things change and we will not be in the same condition all the time. In the words of the Greek philosopher Heraclitus, "Everything flows and nothing abides; everything gives way and nothing stays fixed." When I had natural childbirth with Alexandra and Brooke, I learned that by focusing on one fixed object I could be awake and aware and control the pain of the contractions. I insisted on natural childbirth because I wanted to be there for the experience of a new life coming into the world. I wanted to feel the moment and the drama fully. I knew that eventually the pain would go away.

You can play a positive role in your healing. How we treat ourselves when we're healing can determine the difference between stagnation and recovery. Patience and acceptance are also crucial. When I first injured my back, I was told that an operation would not be as beneficial as letting it heal naturally. I asked the doctor how long it would take to heal. He told me he wasn't certain; it could take six weeks or six months. To aid in my recovery, I rented a massage table, set it up in our bedroom, and every other day a message therapist came to work on me. I healed in a little over a month.

It's particularly important to take action on your own behalf, to do things that not only physically encourage your healing but to do little things that lift your spirits. When I slipped my disc and was flat on my back, I lay on the floor because I learned that staying in bed was depressing. Staying in bed made me feel mentally off. To lift myself up, I would dress in colorful tights and a freshly ironed blouse, even though my destination was the bedroom floor. This never failed to help my morale. My doctor was sympathetic to this holistic perspective on health. He agreed that staying in bed could weaken instead of strengthen me. Sitting in a chair, reading, looking out the window can be just the thing that gives us the lift we need when we have back pain, a bad cold, or the flu.

There are any number of daily rituals that can help restore us and bring us back to our essence. Think about the simple things you can do for yourself that bring comfort and spiritual healing.

Rest and relaxation can bring great results. Whenever you practice deep relaxation, whether through yoga, meditation, biofeedback, or just resting in a hammock or your favorite club chair, you will be refreshed even when you feel ill. I revive myself by taking these minibreaks. Peter and I often take a two-minute rest where we put our heads back and close our eyes. There are exercises you can do to relax yourself by concentrating on your breathing or visualizing an image. When the children were young and couldn't fall asleep, Peter would tell them they were each a fifty-pound bag of potatoes in a burlap sack with a hole in the bottom. He'd tell them to visualize the potatoes falling out, little by little. I like to visualize natural beauty. The more alert you are to images that calm you, the more easily you can conjure them up and relax into them.

The best [man] is like water. Water is good; it benefits all things and does not compete with them.

LAO-TZU

Each of us finds a way to unwind. Peter and I love to go to our special bistro because not only is the food good, but it is where Peter proposed to me. Over the past twenty years we've enjoyed seeing the same waiters as well as the other regular customers. Through the years we've watched one man in his own healing process. He always dines alone. But he loves good food and eats ceremoniously. Between small bites he takes a sip of wine, puts his glass down, reaches both arms across the white tablecloth, and rests for an indefinite time. He never rushes. Sometimes, just watching this man's pleasure calms me.

Relaxing is a gentle art that puts us in charge of ourself all the time. Clearing the mind produces a deep state of restful alertness that is rejuvenating.

I have learned that there are many things that can help me cope with pain and illness. I'd like to share some of them with you.

Doing for Others Perhaps our greatest opportunity to heal comes when we focus on the ways in which we are all part of a larger world and when we do whatever we can to connect to others to make all of our lives better. Understanding our human connection to others releases us from the loneliness of being ill.

I knew then that "w-a-t-e-r" meant the wonderful cool something that was flowing over my hand. That living word awakened my soul, gave it light, joy, set it free!

HELEN KELLER

Helping others and bringing whatever light we can to the world takes us out of ourselves and away from our problems. Giving to others widens our perspective and enlarges our empathy.

We learn the wisdom of "It's better to give than to receive" by our actions. We can always find inventive ways to "give back," even if life is busy and money is tight. It's paradoxical how powerfully healing giving is. It not only gets you outside of yourself; it throws you into a more empathetic consciousness. You feel useful, needed because there is someone's heart you are able to touch. Whenever you do anything with the pure intention of helping another human soul, you are immediately rewarded. Caring for others requires that you give of yourself, in your own way, freely, purely, genuinely. But by doing so, you're nurturing your soul as well.

A young single journalist signed up at a local hospital to be a godmother to an ex-drug addict. She visited Denise regularly, helped her do the shopping, played with the children, did their laundry, and once a month took the family—Denise and her two boys—to the movies. Brenda took these kids out of their treeless, inner-city neighborhood into public parks, where they'd have festive picnics and explore. Eric, the nine-year-old, had never smelled a daffodil before one of their outings.

Live close to nature who will teach the essential lessons of change and letting go.

Cindy, a middle-aged, middle-class mother of five children, "adopted" a Mexican migrant family from a neighboring county in California fifteen years ago. For many years she has watched over this family of six children and their father, providing them with everything from Thanksgiving meals to books, clothes, nights at the movies, and even swimming lessons. My brother Powell's favorite charity in Chicago was the "Off the Street Club," where three thousand boys and girls are given a chance for a better life. His children remember delivering toys to children they never knew at Christmastime, as well as having some boys and girls from "the club" gather around their dining room table for Sunday dinners.

A friend who is about to go into the hospital for surgery is being helped by people who offer to do her grocery shopping, walk her dog, and run errands for her, including car pool. When my mother died, Peter's sister Bebe didn't ask what she could do, she just arrived at my Aunt Susie's house with three huge platters of delicious salads. We don't need an invitation to give to others.

Eleanor McMillen Brown suffered a long illness before she died. For the eight years that Mrs. Brown was in a coma, Peter and I would go visit her once a week, usually Sunday afternoon. While we initially went to give companionship to my mentor and friend, we realized that her caring, devoted nurses enjoyed our visits and looked forward to them because we were able to bring some news and laughter to Mrs. Brown's quiet apartment.

What are some of the ways you like to give to others? Even though my daughter Alexandra rarely eats her own baked goods, she makes carrot cakes and takes them to a sick friend or to someone recovering from surgery in the hospital. We know a large family in China and enjoy packing up bundles of clothes several times a year and sending them off to Beijing. Sometimes we receive pictures of the family smiling, wearing the items we've sent them.

There is something infinitely healing in the repeated refrains of nature—the assurance that dawn comes after night, and spring after winter.

RACHEL CARSON

I tend to write a sympathy letter to someone I know who is suffering. When I receive such tender notes from loved ones, it always helps me to remember that I am being thought of and that someone else cares about my pain.

There is always something you can do for others to make something positive of your pain. It can be anything from the simplest thing like writing these letters, to tell someone you care, to giving generously of yourself during a tragedy. When Margaret and Reginald Green were on a family vacation in Italy with their two children, Nicholas, seven, and Eleanor, four, they were driving along a highway when a small car followed them and bandits opened fire, shooting and killing Nicholas who was sleeping in the backseat of the car. As the world wept over this tragedy, the Greens resolved to honor their son's memory by donating his organs which were later given to seven recipients. The Greens won a gold medal from the mayor of Rome for this generous donation. "The decision to donate his organs was spontaneous and heartfelt," said Mr. Green in an article in *The New York Times*. "Our little guy was going to have a great future. That's been taken away. Now somebody else ought to have a shot at it." After Nicholas's funeral, his father said, "All the human sympathy that's come our way has changed this into something more profound—more spiritual, in a way. I have a vision of millions of parents all over the world giving their children just a slightly longer hug before sending them off to school, and reading one extra page before they go to bed at night."

How beautiful is the rain!
HENRY WADSWORTH LONGFELLOW

Extraordinary acts of grace like this can redeem us and heal our pain. When we rise above ourselves this way, we feel less alone in our suffering and are buoyed up by knowing we have made a difference in the lives of others. It also takes us away from our own problems.

Making Sure You Have a Caring Doctor "Virtue is like health: the harmony of the whole man," insisted Thomas Carlyle, the nineteenth-century British essayist. A doctor who looks at your health in terms of your whole self—your body, your mind, and your emotional life—is the key to getting good care when you are sick. We are fortunate to have such a doctor.

I personally prefer not to take drugs or extreme measures when I'm ill, and our doctor is very sympathetic to that approach. This is my own preferred strategy. It cannot, however, always be used. Medicine is often a critical ingredient to our healing and we should explore whatever treatment is suggested to us with as much awareness as we can and by trusting our doctors. Practicing preventive medicine by having the right checkups and taking care of yourself is important. Having a caring doctor who doesn't overreact every time you have medical symptoms is also essential to the practice of good preventive medicine.

When I hear music, I fear no danger. I am invulnerable. I see no foe. I am related to the earliest times, and to the latest.

HENRY DAVID THOREAU

Taking the Water Cure The first place I head when I'm feeling run-down is to water. Water plays a major role in preventing illness and maintaining good health and wellness.

Water is healing. Life comes from the water; our bodies are approximately 90 percent water. Millions of years ago, we're told, we were little cells drifting around in the water. Today we feel the ebbing and flowing of the tides as an ancient song that moves to our own inner rhythms. My godmother, Mitzi Christian, felt she could accomplish anything she wanted to do when she was breathing in sea air. Years ago, I met a friend who earned extra money taking a cumbersomely large woman to the beach. He helped her to the water's edge and, while she sat with her feet in the cold, wet sand, he threw buckets of cold ocean water all over her, from head to toe. She loved it. It lifted her spirits. To her it was a cure. My friend moved me when he told me how she would howl with joy every time she touched water. Water is cleansing and calming. It soothes and stimulates us all at the same time. And it's everywhere. If you're landlocked and can afford a beach or lake vacation, head to the water. You will be guaranteed to heal.

Who hears music, feels his solitude / Peopled at once.

ROBERT BROWNING

I recently met a woman who teaches canoeing to juvenile delinquents. "All I have to do is get these great kids out in a canoe on the water to know how good they are inside. I blame their parents and I never need to know what their children did wrong. I wish I had known them earlier."

But you don't have to be near huge quantities of water to get benefits from it. You can get what you need of it in your own home. When I'm feeling worn down, there is nothing like a bath to restore me. While many people adore their living room sofa, I prefer my bathtub. I speak so rhapsodically of these glorious baths that when I wrote *Living a Beautiful Life*, the copy editor made notes in the manuscript's margin saying, "Oh, no, not another bath!" But when you consider all our daily rituals of eating, sleeping, and washing, water plays a very significant part in our lives. I love to draw a cool bath, undress, and lie there with the window wide open, in the late afternoon, following some time in the garden. The bathroom in our cottage is plain and small, but the window facing west is heavenly. I lean my head back in our deep, old, footed tub and have a five-minute soak. When I close my eyes, I can be anywhere. Letting your mind wander into fantasy is a wonderful way to relax and heal. Where better to do so than in a tub of water?

In China the patient is responsible for helping to prevent illness or maintain health. . . Try to center yourself and feel balanced.

DR. DAVID EISENBERG

A glass of hot water with a squirt of lemon in it, first thing when you wake up in the morning, is good for your circulation. I know people who drink several quarts of water a day and spray mineral water on their faces as their only beauty aids.

Making Life Beautiful The second most-useful aid to healing after water is beauty. Beauty can be found everywhere. There is beauty in the natural world and beauty that's made by human hands. Beauty produces pleasure and is therapeutic to our spirit. Beauty creates a positive state in us. Beauty increases our ability to appreciate life, to feel more rather than know more, which in turn increases our ability to care for others and to love. Beauty awakens me to what is positive in life. It is always there for the taking.

One listless Sunday in July, I felt weak and achy and had trouble concentrating at my desk. Rather than wasting time in a muddle, I decided to go outside. There I saw our antique red wheelbarrow brimming with yellow and purple pansies, lots of brightly colored lilies, and our new friend, a male red cardinal, observing his brown mate building a nest in the trellis of the fence. I watered, pruned, clipped, mowed the lawn, and swept the path to our tiny backyard. I picked several-dozen pansies, put them in a small white pitcher with a rope design on the handle, and arranged the flowers. I clipped some sprigs of mint for my iced tea, sliced open an orange, squeezed the juice into my tea, selected a fun, handblown glass, put a silver sipper in the glass, poured in the tea over lots of clear ice cubes, and ran upstairs with the drink and a pitcher of pansies. I was a different person. All my dull symptoms were gone. Being active, not only in nature, but anywhere, can relieve most of my aches and pains.

Beauty may not take away all the hurt, but slowly, it can replace it with joy. The more joy we experience, the better we are able to cope with the loss of it. Beauty is transcendent.

Beauty takes us away from our pain. That's why the environment in which we are ill is so important to our recovery. Aesthetically speaking, a hospital is the last place a sick person should be. I have read recently, though, that architects and planners are becoming more sensitive to the need for a beautiful, comforting environment for those who are not well. Let's hope that more institutions will be built with that in mind.

Where can we look for beauty in our everyday lives?

I find that having color around me always lifts my spirits. Color cheers, soothes, and delights us. I'm often cheered up when I use an elastic band in my hair that is spring green or bright pink or lemon yellow. Everything from choosing a sky-blue paper clip, writing with a pretty ink color, using a bright-yellow pen, to holding my papers down with a lovely, colorful glass paperweight can make me feel better. Anything that delights us will speed us along on the path to healing.

It's been documented that certain colors contribute to our

Happiness is the criterion of excellence in the art of living. . . The opposite of happiness thus is not grief or pain but depression which results from inner sterility and unproductiveness.

ERICH FROMM

moods in a significant way. Some colors bring our mood down and may have a depressant effect. There are cheerful colors and colors that can whisper calmly, too.

Vitality! That's the pursuit of life, isn't it?

KATHARINE HEPBURN

Color affects us each individually. Your favorite hues reflect your inner self and can be extremely therapeutic. At the same time, certain colors can dampen your spirits. All mousy colors make me sad. I can't cope with taupe. Certain colors remind me of dead insects; others make me think of the uniforms worn in the Vietnam War. Different colors work on us emotionally, depending on our personality and our likes and dislikes. Generally, each color in the color wheel has a reputation for being lively or calm, depending on where it is located.

Red is the most aggressive color, full of fire and energy. Red is strong, increases your heartbeat, is powerful and not for sissies.

Yellow is the sunshine, the happiest color, optimistic and perky. Yellow smiles at you and is welcoming.

Green means new life, renewal, spring, freshness. Green is relaxing, makes us think of nature, nurture, and being grounded.

Blue is peaceful, meditative, and mature. Blue calms us, lowers our heart rate, and is relaxing. Many bedrooms are blue because the color is conducive to serenity and sleep.

Woe brings woe upon woe.

SOPHOCLES

I've been a colorist ever since I was three and in love with my mother's garden. The clearer, fresher, cleaner the color, the happier it makes me. The more delicate and pure the tint, the more positively it affects my psyche. I keep color pencils on my desk as well as crayons with the wrapping taken off them so I can see their energetic hues in all their glory. Bright, cheerful colors, whether they are on a candle, a Post-it Note, a piece of stationery, a file folder, an umbrella, a silk scarf, or a necktie, uplift my spirits.

When you are going through a difficult time, colors can improve your mood. Make a deliberate effort to select a favorite pink napkin or a soft lilac bathrobe or some red socks or yellow Wellington boots. So many things can be selected in a preferred color, from the handle of scissors to ribbons, a toothbrush, and even a bar of soap or a sponge. You can surround yourself with all the colors that you love. In sad times, these colors will carry you along, be at your side, and silently let you know you are healing.

I shall allow no man to belittle my soul by making me hate him.

BOOKER T. WASHINGTON

A woman who enlisted me to decorate her home told me she was experiencing terrible burnout in her professional life and she needed a soothing atmosphere to return to at night. Her beige apartment was definitely dulling her senses. I sensed that Barbara was depressed, and from my initial interview with her, I felt she was unable to snap out of her gloom without some help. Even the lighting in her rooms was dim, and there were beige, limp undercurtains drawn across all the windows, adding to the dismal feel. Barbara lived on two acres and didn't have any neighbors in sight, yet she felt the need to hide.

Listening to her I realized she was experiencing severe inner turmoil. Home was like a strong tranquilizer. Barbara slept most of the time when she wasn't working at the office.

While looking at color swatches, paint books, fabric samples, tiles, rug samples, and pictures of room interiors, I saw some enthusiasm rise out of Barbara. Together we opened some doors to help unlock her pain. We began in her bedroom, replacing the beige with bright, sparkling-white walls and white cotton dotted-swiss curtains. We painted the ceiling "Atmosphere Blue," we lightened the floors by pickling the oak, and we used yellow-and-white-striped sheets on her bed, adding extra white pillows and a quilted, white-eyelet comforter. At the foot of Barbara's bed we draped a French-blue mohair throw. Behind the bed we hung a patchwork quilt of yellow, white, and blue.

Barbara is generous in her praise of how this color scheme has snapped her out of her depression. Maybe just the realization that she needed to pay more attention to her private life helped her to regain her vitality and balance.

Peter and I feel color deprivation when we travel and stay in a hotel room that is beige. It has the same effect as a dark, dreary day. Color, when properly understood, can boost us into feeling more energy and therefore more joy.

When Peter and I painted our apartment living room "Perfect Yellow," his brother George looked around and announced, "I hate yellow." I told this story at a seminar where we discussed the delights of color in every room of the house. Everyone laughed. But, as I explained to them, everyone's sense of color is different. It isn't always possible to please anyone but yourself and your family. My colors are clear, bright, and child-like because, frankly, that's what suits me, cheers me, and makes me feel good. Other people understand these clear hues as a vital expression of my personality. I'm fortunate that Peter and our children thrive on the same garden-fresh hues. Peter often tells me the colors he experiences every day soothe his heartbeat.

Filling your home with colors you love creates a happy environment. Caring about your home, wanting to feel a sense of pleasure from your time spent there, alone as well as with family and friends, is extremely healing. By having reverence for the small, simple, often obvious, yet enormously useful, things we do to change our environment for

Love yourself as your neighbor.

LAURA HUXLEY

the better, we get back in touch with ourselves. Obviously, cheerful colors and fresh flowers aren't enough to guarantee that we will get sick less, but they can play some part in the healing and preventive processes.

Soothing with Laughter One of the greatest gifts we possess is the gift of laughter. Laughter is instrumental in healing. I'm reminded of Norman Cousins watching the Marx Brothers when he was sick in the hospital, as recounted in his *Anatomy of an Illness*. Whenever I'm sad, my body becomes heavy, I find everything an effort, I feel weak, and everything seems so serious. Laughter brings release. Laughter brings balance. After a hard cry, I want someone to make me laugh so I can relieve some of the sadness and feel renewed.

It is neither wealth nor splendor, but tranquility and occupation, which give happiness.

THOMAS JEFFERSON

Laughter is always appropriate when you are healing. When Brooke is going through a tough time, she'll go to the library in our apartment and watch one of her favorite television shows. Peter and I can hear her chuckle several rooms away. What usually happens whenever I cry is I end up laughing away my tears. Sadness and sorrow need to be balanced with lightheartedness. Laughter is regenerative. Of all animals, only humans distinguish themselves with laughter. The more pain we feel, the greater the need to laugh.

From my own experience and from observing my family and friends, laughter is essential at the most agonizing times because we literally laugh so we won't weep. We get the giggles over the stupidest little things, and laugh uncontrollably. Our body is glad to take some of the lead away. The poet Shelley reminds us that "Our sincerest laughter/with some pain is fraught;/Our sweetest songs are those/that tell of saddest thought."

Whenever we laugh, the world laughs with us. When we're experiencing an excess of sorrow, paradoxically, laughing will help us heal. Long faces never help us accept reality and adjust to our circumstances. A hospital in Colorado has a sign in the waiting room telling visitors they cannot go beyond the glass door where they visit patients unless they are cheerful. Make me laugh when I'm in pain and you'll help me to heal.

Reading Inspiring Literature Literature is an essential companion in times of suffering, pain, illness, and sorrow. We are powerfully influenced by what we read. Whenever I need healing, I read serious literature. I don't read to escape. I read to deepen and to grow more knowing. Books can open doors of experience. I owe so much of my contentment to identifying with writers through their works. When you read beautifully written books, your experience is validated and made into something bigger than yourself, something enobling. Many times you discover that you are not alone in your pain. You read and think, *Yes, this is true. That is how I feel.* It can be an affirmation of your humanity.

The beauty of language, the thoughts, wisdom, and enlightenment we gain while reading great books widens our understanding of life. When you read, it's good to be unusually open to any new insights. Be flexible and spontaneous so the words have an opportunity to change reality for you. Have a reading list ready when you are well so it will be handy when you are ill. This way, you can start the healing process immediately. Try new authors. Read and reread the classics. Push yourself beyond what you are used to reading and stretch yourself. It also helps to ask people what they're reading—what stimulates them intellectually, what illuminates them spiritually.

Yesterday, a shaft of light cut into the darkness.

JOHN F. KENNEDY

The summer of my sixteenth year, my aunt Betty sent me fifty-four books and insisted I read them before going around the world with her four months later. Since that time, I've read a vast repertoire of books going back to the Greeks and Romans. I devour whatever insights I find. That's why I feel so strongly about censorship. Books should never be banned. Not from library shelves or bookstores. Regardless of content, the freedom of the written word is one of our birthrights and it should never be taken from us under any circumstances. By reading about things both alien and familiar to us we develop an understanding of how others live and feel, even if we do not find their lives akin to our own. Usually, when a writer has a message that's written from the heart, there's something in those pages that can help us. When we resist change or a new perspective, we will not continue to grow, and as a culture, we will surely die.

We're trying to cultivate the soil of those inner resources in people and help them to realize— that is, make real in their lives—that they can bring mindfulness, concentration, calmness, and clear seeing into the moment-to-moment stuff of life.

DR. JON KABAT-ZINN

Music Soothes the Soul Music and other beautiful sounds are another great source of healing. When I listen to really great music I feel uplifted, enabled, and inspired. While I don't consider myself musical (I have no talent for playing instruments or singing), I have an enormous appreciation for the beauty of good music. Growing up I played the clarinet, trumpet, piano, and I sang in church and school choirs. I was dreadfully off. In my senior year in high school, I founded "The Off Keys" singing group. Several of my good friends and I entertained the student body with our lack of ability.

Music, when it stirs my essence, cuts through time, place and circumstance. Some of my personal favorites, the sounds of ceremonies, make me cry with tenderness and grace. I love to hear the graduation "Pomp and Circumstance" marches by Edward Elgar and all wedding music. The prettiest composition to me is the "Trumpet Voluntary" by Jeremiah Clarke, which never fails to give me chills. I also love the more festive wedding pieces, the

Wagner processional from *Lohengrin* known to us as "Here Comes the Bride," and Mendelssohn's recessional wedding march commissioned as incidental music for a production of Shakespeare's *A Midsummer Night's Dream.* Sounds are full of memories, like Tchaikovsky's music for *The Nutcracker.* We took Alexandra and Brooke to this ballet every Christmas season at Lincoln Center. When the Mormon Tabernacle Choir sings "O Holy Night," I dissolve. Whether Nat King Cole or his daughter Natalie sings "Unforgettable," I get all sentimental, nostalgic, and feel warm inside. And "Old Blue Eyes," Frank Sinatra, is loved by our parents' generation as well as our children's. Often when I read for pleasure, I'll put on some of his tapes and escape into a youthful "warm September of my years." Handel's *Messiah*; Hubert Parry's "Jerusalem" (from *Chariots of Fire*); Mozart's *Requiem*; the sound of Harry Belafonte's voice; and Enya's *Watermark*, all delight my spirits.

Healing emanates from the heart.

PETER MEGARGEE BROWN

Often when I write I listen to Danny Wright at the piano. The background music inspires me without distracting my concentration. My favorite instrumental is from Beethoven's Seventh Symphony. It's so moving, inspirational, yet sad, powerful and poignant. I become so wrapped up in this experience, I feel I have been transported into a transcending state of grace and love.

Singing songs, hymns, or carols with friends fills us with a sense of beautiful community. Singing, like laughing, is good for the soul. It's impossible to feel rage when you are singing.

I always appreciate any sound that moves me. Birds, the sound of the waves crashing to the shore, the sound of children laughing, all compose the healing music of our everyday lives. The sizzle of olive oil in the frying pan, water boiling, the sound of a crackling fire, and the sound of chimes and ticking clocks fill me with a sense of the great bounty of life. In our village, I love to hear the sounds of halyards and the lines of the sails flapping against each other, and the church bells and marching bands in summer.

A man must learn to endure that patiently which he cannot avoid conveniently.

MICHEL DE MONTAIGNE

Sound has a way of bypassing our critical mind and going straight to our heart. Perhaps that is why conductors and musicians are known to live long, healthy lives.

Delightful Aromas Anything that fills you with the greatness and the richness of life will help you cope with illness and, ultimately, it will heal you. I'm increasingly alert to how powerful the influence of smell is to my mood, as are my other senses. Aromatherapy can be enormously healing. By becoming more aware of how important smells can be to us and to those we love, we can pay closer attention to those scents that soothe our spirits, and those that we detest. We've had several skunks in our village recently and the lingering odor of their spray makes me feel faint. When a skunk does its number, even a restaurant full of romantic diners, sizzling butter, grilled chicken and fish can't take away this overpoweringly wretched smell. A skunk has the power to be overbearing.

We must counterbalance the vile odors we're exposed to with favorite, happy smells that have positive associations. What are some scents that fill you with pleasure? Ask anyone you love and each person will have scents he or she feels passionate about that are often rooted in memories of childhood or connected to loving relationships with others. While my sense of sight is the most important of my five senses, I can envision a beautiful vista even with my eyes shut. But a good smell can delight us and a repugnant one can cause us to feel sick.

Good smells sharpen my passions. Just as some people enjoy

colors that make me sad, some smells I adore could make some-one else feel faint. Reactions to smells are personal. I enjoy the scent of beeswax, for example, so these candles bring me added pleasure beyond the color and design. My friend Julie loves the smell of sagebrush on cold, crisp mornings in Wyoming. But I've never been to Wyoming! All my favorite smells trigger memories that empower them with symbolism and bring flashbacks of happy times during my growing up.

One of the greatest scents is the smell of breakfast. When you're upstairs, cuddled under fresh linen sheets, cozy in bed, and you smell bacon, eggs, toast, hot chocolate, and coffee, you're filled with anticipation and a feeling that you're loved. As a child, I loved mornings when my parents lit a fire in our dining room. There's something so primitive and satisfying about the smell of firewood crackling in a hearth. I love walking in our village in the fall and winter months smelling the wood burning in many of the houses in our neighborhood.

The smell of sea air fills my lungs with vitality. Early morning dew with crisp air brings me back to first grade when I'd run barefoot to my garden to discover what had ripened or grown in the night. Whether it's the earthy smell of a horse barn, sassafras, birch beer, honeysuckle, pine trees, or the burning of fall leaves, I feel young again and am awake to a flood of vivid images and memories. I can smell bubble gum and remember going out behind the bushes in Newport, Rhode Island, when I was five, when my sister and brother and I had a bubble-gum contest. Although I ended up with bubble gum in my hair and eyebrows that day, the excitement of the pink gum is fresh in my mind almost fifty years later.

The word "health" itself is so interesting because it comes from a root that means "whole." Part of being a healthy person is being well integrated and at peace, with all of the systems acting together.

DR. CANDACE PERT

I love the smell of waxed floors and furniture. New York has pretzel and roasted chestnut smells. Movie theaters smell of popcorn. Grinding coffee beans brings pleasure before you've had your first sip of coffee in the morning. Slicing open a few oranges and making freshly squeezed juice is a sensuous delight. Johnson's baby powder is the next-best thing to smelling the heavenly scent of a baby. I love the smell of boiling apples with cloves and cinnamon. I'd rather smell apple crisp than taste it. Hot chocolate-chip cookies fresh out of the oven smell like life is indeed worth living.

Freshly baked bread smells so good I forget to exhale. A host of daffodils in spring stirs in me thoughts of a freshness so pure and magnificent it permeates my soul as though I were sitting on a moist rock after a light rainfall, in a field, surrounded by these yellow trumpets heralding joy. Gardenias intoxicate me to such a degree I can't think clearly when I'm in a room with them. The smell of the incense piñon takes me to Santa Fe, where I can also appreciate the scent of mesquite wood burning and the fresh air that turns me inside out.

I enjoy the smell of fresh butter, grape jelly, lilac, Chinese restaurants; the smell of my writing paper, the ink flowing from my pen, the small strawberry tart I treat myself to with my peppermint tea, the mint, the vanilla candle; so sweet are the sugar cookie, the jasmine soap, fresh-mown grass, almond oil, lily of the valley from the garden. And lemons. When Peter and I first dated, I wore Love Fresh Lemon cologne. Few smells are as appealing to me as lemons.

The feast of reason and the flow of soul.

ALEXANDER POPE

Just as people have a certain smell to them, so do houses. I find it pleasant to be able to experience so many favorite smells in a home. From the potpourri, the bath gel, the scent of sheets, and, of course, the smells coming from the kitchen, home can be a haven where aromatherapy is a deliberate way for you to help your healing.

Spiritual Healing

There is far more to our sense of health than we may be aware of. Getting in touch with our deep spiritual energies, our *ch'i*, has a powerful effect on our health. When we can learn to be still within ourselves, we will grow more in touch with our essence, our life force. When I sit in silence on my stone meditation bench in our Zen garden, I can feel something stirring deep within me. We can deliberately bring ourselves to this place when we take time for "concentrated meditation," a concept described by philosopher and psychoanalyst Erich Fromm in his 1956 classic, *The Art of Loving.* According to Fromm, if we concentrate with our whole being on the qualities that make life rich, if we meditate on the meaning and value of life, visualizing goals and having dreams, we can, to a far greater degree than we can prove scientifically, direct and redirect our energies toward wholeness.

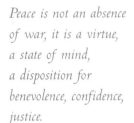

Peace is not an absence of war, it is a virtue, a state of mind, a disposition for benevolence, confidence, justice.

SPINOZA

When we set up our lives in such a way that we have time and place for ourselves, this stillness, like a beautiful breeze, comes and renews us. When we feel this we are in touch with a resonance, a vibration of the essential life force within us. After a while, we come to recognize this feeling as our very life blood, the source of all our strength. Stillness opens us to our essential energy. It is a place of innocence where we gain a sense of wonder. We experience ourselves and our connection to everything that lives. We feel at one with the universe. When we take a deep breath and let it go, we can connect to this vital spiritual energy.

In the compassionate words of the present Dalai Lama of Tibet, "There is too much emphasis on what is minor and not on what is essential. And what is essential involves being able to transform the individual from within." The Dalai Lama urges us to bring about our own inner transformation and healing.

You cannot put the same shoe on every foot.

PUBLILIUS SYRUS

But many people are too locked into what is tangible and measurable to open up to this invisible force within each of us. I had a startling experience of this one evening when a friend told me that she went to a lecture given by Thomas Moore, author of *Care of the Soul.* Halfway through the evening, one member of the audience became more and more anxious and frustrated, raising his hand to ask three curious questions: "How much does the soul weigh? Where is it in the human body? What does it look like?" Moore paused to wait for the laughter of the audience to subside, then he quietly said, "I don't know." Furious, the man got up and left the auditorium. Apparently he could not deal with the mystery and abstraction of the concept of a soul. The soul simply did not exist for him if it could not be measured.

But there is indeed a spiritual dimension to our lives. And it is particularly available to us when we are ill. When our power is diminished, we are forced to give up trying to control everything. We are, in a way, free of that expectation. This time of enforced stillness allows us to absorb energy and awareness from the universe. When we make a commitment to develop our spiritual dimension, we discover opportunities to connect to this life force everywhere. By not resisting what we don't understand or what is unknown, we open ourselves to life's infinite possibilities.

This nation cannot afford to be materially rich and spiritually poor.

JOHN F. KENNEDY

When we communicate with ourselves deeply, we connect to this aspect of our lives. Listening to ourselves when we are alone takes us to this path as well. "Listening," as psychoanalyst Theodor Reik wrote, "with a third ear is one of the most important tools necessary to orchestrate a pleasant balance in our lives." Our beliefs and actions must be compatible.

I can listen to myself when I am alone and uninterrupted. I try to build these listening times into my day, no matter where I am or what my schedule may be. When I listen with an open heart, my intuition is strong and I can see truth on a more spiritual plane. Being still and paying attention is important to understanding what is good for ourselves alone. By focusing on this energy, we can channel it to good places. The divine law of the universe is that each of us can learn from our experiences, especially the painful ones, and redirect our energy so it is transformed into positive, loving, and compassionate actions for ourselves and others. Giving to others can also put us in touch with this universal energy. When we are committed to this path, everything feeds the well.

The beauty of the world has two edges, one of laughter, one of anguish...

VIRGINIA WOOLF

Giving, being useful, caring about others, finding our purpose, all of these are the ingredients to a spiritually healthy life. When we open our hearts, letting more love in, gradually we feel more acceptance, and acceptance brings healing. And while others can help us to heal ourselves, the real healing is up to each individual soul.

It may seem intimidating to follow this path, this energy, but it is not hard to begin the process of healing by connecting to your spiritual self. As Lao-tzu said, "The journey of a thousand miles begins with one step." This has been my healing mantra and has helped me to take many small but important steps along the way to good health.

5

Death

"Alexandra, I am going to a party and you are *not* invited."

— MOTHER, on her deathbed

Have a wonderful new year filled with joy, peace, love, adventure, mystery, miracles, and good health!

—BROTHER POWELL,
in a letter to me four weeks before his death

Living with Death

The fact of our own death is known only to human beings. Animals may sense danger when they are being hunted by their natural enemies, but a lion does not know that some day, inevitably, he will die. Human beings know this about their lives, and this extraordinary knowledge informs and shapes our whole existence. But this knowledge is not only a source of fear and pain; it also serves a greater good. Death teaches us about what is deeply within our nature: an ability to accept our lack of control and feel ourselves one with something larger than ourselves, the universe. Death reminds us that we do not have ultimate control over our lives. With that knowledge comes a certain freedom. Knowing that our limitations are part of our destiny frees us of the need to resist our own nature, which is imperfect. We cannot try to be perfect; only death in its finality is perfect. And the finality of death allows us a deep appreciation for the value of our lives and the lives of those we love.

The memory of you with those you left behind is perhaps your ultimate immortality.

PETER MEGARGEE BROWN

Many mystics, meditation gurus, and spiritual leaders agree that death is the greatest teacher of life. Eknath Easwaran, the Indian philosopher, teacher, and writer, explains why. Death "throws life into the sharpest perspective, pressing us to achieve our fullest potential." It seems that to redeem our lives in the face of death we know we must live more fully while we can. The author of *The Tibetan Book of Living and Dying*, Sogyal Rinpoche, assures us we will all die successfully. It will be perfect. He urges us to take death seriously and to see life as a whole that includes death. We are all going to die. That is the only certainty.

We live in a society in denial of death. We try to fool ourselves into thinking we are invulnerable. We look for reassurance that we are not merely mortal in the things we buy, in always trying to look younger, get stronger, and remake ourselves. In all of this we can see that we are trying desperately to deny that this life ends. As long as there is a new trend tomorrow, we feel somehow that life will keep renewing itself and we will never die. This denial compromises the real depth of experience we can have in our lives. "In a world that denies death," writes Thomas Moore in his book *Care of the Soul*, "vitality, too, may fade, for death and life are two sides of one coin."

But by facing our mortality head-on, we can live more vividly on every level. A lot of richness can be added to our lives by acknowledging our death. Doing so enables us to live life more fully. A lot of unnecessary suffering, too, could be avoided by an understanding of the process of death, our final loss of control.

Death is not always painless. As long as we are alive and can feel, we will feel pain. But that pain gives our life meaning and dimension. There is a terrible sadness at the thought of the deaths of those we love. Yet whenever someone dies, the event sharpens our appreciation of what it means to be alive, to have a body. To be able to watch a sunset, to tenderly touch a loved one, to play hopscotch with a grandchild, to taste Maine lobster and corn on the cob in July, to look up at the sky, the moon, the stars, to experience the sea, to climb a mountain, are all delights of the living. We do not know what happens after death.

In my beginning is my end.

T. S. ELIOT

We may some day catch an abstract truth by the tail, and then we shall have our religion and our immortality.

HENRY ADAMS

Death is actually a familiar figure in our lives. We experience it in different incarnations each day. When things change in our lives, we feel the loss of what we had before as a kind of death. Following that "death," we pass through a time of confusion about how our lives will begin anew. Somehow, this experience makes death feel intimate, familiar, even when we have never had any experience with it ourselves. "There is no place on earth where death cannot find us," wrote my favorite essayist, sixteenth-century French writer, Michel de Montaigne. "We do not know where death awaits us; so let us wait for it everywhere. To practice death is to practice freedom." I think that what Montaigne meant by this was much what Elisabeth Kübler-Ross speaks of when she says:

> "Dying is something we human beings do continuously, not just at the end of our physical lives on this earth. The stages of dying apply equally to any significant change, e.g., retirement, moving to a new city, changing jobs, divorce; change is a regular occurrence in human existence. If you can face and understand your ultimate death, perhaps you can learn to face and deal productively with each change that presents itself in your life."

Indeed, there is great freedom in accepting and understanding death.

How Do We Live with Death?

When my friend Tess, a professional photographer, was dying of cancer in Memorial Sloan-Kettering Cancer Center, she took up painting, since she could no longer lift her photography equipment. She brought her watercolors to bed with her and continued painting. One December Saturday afternoon, Tess broke down in tears. "I'm not going to make it, am I?" Taken aback by this aching question, I cried for a second, then laughed, "No, but neither am I." Why is it, I wonder, that laughter appears during tragedy? On my way to the hospital I had picked up a little two-inch azure blue wood box. When the lid of the box is opened, up pops a little mother doll holding her daughter, draped in a Liberty of London floral cotton print. It really made me laugh when I saw it in the store. I had anxiously struggled to open the box, so nervous about Tess. But the box made Tess laugh, too. Perhaps on that snowy day a good laugh was most appropriate. The Russian author Leo Tolstoy once said, "Pure and complete sorrow is as impossible as pure and complete joy."

Two months later, Tess died in Morocco. She had moved out of the hospital, went off to an exotic land of color, light, and spice, with her family, to live, love, and laugh until she stopped breathing. Her husband, Don, told me she affectionately threw a pillow at him hours before she died. There was laughter and love alongside the sorrow.

One way to discover what you want from your life is by writing your epitaph or obituary. Doing this can be a breakthrough experience. After you die, how do you want to be remembered? What insights have you learned that you want to pass on to others? What words do you live by? What truths guide your quest? My epitaph could be ONWARD AND UPWARD. Whatever I leave behind should be upbeat. I like to think of myself as an enabler, someone who helps others live up to their unique potential. The

So minutes, hours, days, months and years /
Pass'd over to the end they were created, /
Would bring white hairs unto a quiet grave. / Ah, what a life were this! how sweet! how lovely!

WILLIAM SHAKESPEARE

usefulness I've experienced will live on and grow in others after I die.

A woman grabbed me after my brother Powell's memorial service. "Sandie, I'm Mary. I used to work for your brother. I'm now a lawyer. He encouraged me to go to law school. He even helped me get in. He told me to go for it. 'Get a seat on the Supreme Court,' he'd tell me. My life is so rich and full because of Powell's encouragement. I just wanted you to know."

For life and death are one, even as the river and the sea are one...

KAHLIL GIBRAN

The obituary you write summing up your life would probably be too subjective to ever appear in any newspaper. Often, the aspects of our life that we value the most, ones that can't be measured tangibly, do not qualify as "successes" in today's society. Caring, loving, helping others to get along in life; the quiet, subtle, yet critical accomplishments of everyday life are not always recognized as important. But most often it is the private gesture, the anonymous gift, the telephone call we make to help a friend, the strong letter of recommendation we write to help a student get into the college of her choice, our devotion to a social cause, the love we show for our family, the nurturing we share with friends and coworkers, that we want to represent our life after we die.

While many of our "good works" are recognized by others, some of the most meaningful moments in life are too personal, too intimate to be well known. Often, rich and powerful people are given long obituaries. I read them with keen interest, wondering how kind and tender this person was. What kind of relationships did he have with his spouse, children, and friends?

When good men die their goodness does not perish,/But lives on though they are gone.

EURIPIDES

After we're dead, we won't sit sipping our morning coffee, reading our obituary. That's not possible. What we can do is write one that will never be published, but one that will be our mantra, words to live by, loving thoughts that guide our path. Maybe we're not president of a large company, but we're the parent of a wonderful child. Writing our epitaph and obituary now, while we're in the stream of life, will help us maintain our balance, keep our priorities in order, and stay focused and steady as we continue our work on earth.

I'm often asked what I want to do with the rest of my life. My answer is clear and consistent: "Exactly what I'm doing now." Be sure your life is up to date, that you are living according to your values, pursuing goals you feel are meaningful. While I was giving a seminar for the University of Tennessee in Chattanooga, there was a conference at the other end of the trade center entitled "The End of the World." At a reception that morning sponsored by the university, several women, disturbed by this dark topic, approached Peter and me. "We'll try to keep these people far away from you, Alexandra. It's so ironic that you're talking about living beautifully and they're discussing the end of the world."

I want death to find me planting my cabbages.

MICHEL DE MONTAIGNE

I laughed and said, "What would you do if the world were to end tonight?" Three of the four women said they wouldn't change anything. The fourth exclaimed, "Oh, no, I'd have to run around and repair all my broken relationships." It's not a bad way to live to greet each new day as if it were the first day of your life and, at the same time, understand that it could be your last. Writing our epitaph and obituary helps us to remain firmly grounded in whatever we believe to be the right life path for us.

Though I am no more expert at death than I am at anything I've never done before, I do think about it a lot and wonder what the right approach to death is. I try to learn from others, still I'm certain I will die feeling ignorant. Life is so complex

When I am dead, my dearest, / Sing no sad songs for me; / Plant thou no roses at my head, / Nor shady cypress tree. / Be the green grass above me / With showers and dewdrops wet; / And if thou wilt, remember / And if thou wilt, forget.

CHRISTINA ROSSETTI

and abundant that a thousand lifetimes wouldn't be enough to sort out the mystery. On his deathbed, our friend Bill (who shared a great vitality with his freshman-year roommate at Princeton, F. Scott Fitzgerald) was too weak to read or speak. When we went to visit him, we heard a tape of Bill's wife and four sons reading his favorite authors to him. They wanted Bill to be hearing his favorite writers and listening to his family's voices. My husband, Peter, wants his own epitaph to read, STILL LEARNING. Bill's life and death continue to teach us how to live with greater awareness.

How can we live well with the certainty of death and the uncertainty of not knowing when or how it will occur? I'm not sure I have the answer, but I do know that by accepting our destiny, we remain more clearly on our path. Elisabeth Kübler-Ross wrote:

> Through a willingness to risk the unknown, to venture forth into unfamiliar territory, you can undertake the search for your own self—the ultimate goal of growth. Through reaching out and committing yourself to dialogue with fellow human beings, you can begin to transcend your individual existence, become at one with yourself and others. And through a lifetime of such commitment, you can face your final end with peace and joy, knowing that you have lived life well.

Everyone has their own way of dealing with death. Some of our methods are born of denial, others come from a religious or spiritual understanding. When someone dies, you often hear people say something euphemistic like, "Henry went to his reward," or "Precious Louise made her transition." I heard a minister one Sunday preaching about resurrection, ending his sermon, "I can hardly wait." When someone dies, so often we're told the person "passed on" to the next world. I know people who believe that their life on earth is only a preparation for the great banquet in the sky. But we don't know for certain that there is life after death, nor do we know if we will return to earth in a new life. What's important is that no matter what exists in the beyond, we are here now, and it is a gift to be alive. Therefore, let us live fully in the present. Find your reasons for living. Live them. Love them. Appreciate them. The world needs each person to play his or her part, to make a contribution.

Death, like birth, is a secret of Nature.

MARCUS AURELIUS

The night before my favorite aunt died, she called thirty-four people. From her hospital bed, family and friends were encouraged to live fully. "What are you having for dinner?" she would ask. "How are the girls? How's your book coming along?" My aunt died while brushing her teeth in bed and glancing at *The New York Times*.

Dr. Lewis Thomas, author of the award-winning *Lives of a Cell*, among other books, was once asked, Is there an art to dying? He replied in an interview with *The New York Times Magazine*:

It is better to learn early of the inevitable depths, for then sorrow and death take their proper place in life, and one is not afraid.

PEARL S. BUCK

There is an art to living. One of the very important things that has to be learned around the time of dying that becomes a real prospect is to recognize those occasions when we have been useful in the world. With the same sharp insight that we all have for acknowledging our failures, we ought to recognize when we have been useful, and sometimes uniquely useful. All of us have had such times in our lives, but we don't pay much attention to them. Yet the thing we're really good at as a species is usefulness. If we paid more attention to this biological attribute, we'd get satisfaction that cannot be attained from goods or knowledge. If you can contemplate the times when you've been useful, even indispensable, to other people, the review of our lives would begin to have effects on the younger generations. Plain usefulness.

What to Do Between Birth and Death

My clairvoyant friend Claire O'Classen suggests we imagine our lives in ten-year increments right up until we're ninety-nine. Most people stop living prematurely. Death reminds us that we won't be here forever. We must therefore do the best we can in the time we're been given and then let go of the impossible, gracefully. When we approach our death with this sense of balance, we will be at peace with ourselves. There are things you can do to bring the positive recognition of death into your life. It's always a good idea to have your affairs in order.

Every parting gives a foretaste of death; every coming together again a foretaste of resurrection.

ARTHUR SCHOPENHAUER

Here are a number of things you should consider doing to make it easier for you and your family to cope with your death:

Your Living Will I hope you will be sure to sign a living will in which you indicate the type of care you would want if you were too ill and couldn't communicate the instructions to your doctors. Assign to someone a health-care power of attorney, someone who can make medical decisions for you in the event that you are temporarily or permanently unable. My mother's living will specified that she did not wish to be indefinitely sustained on mechanical life support. I don't want any heroic measures taken when I am in the dying process. But everyone is different. The living will spells out your personal wishes and relieves loved ones of the guilt and uncertainty of having to make such a difficult decision without you, never knowing if you would have wanted it or not. A living will is a loving and responsible act on our part for our loved ones.

Your Will One way to relax about your own death is to keep your records up-to-date. Even if you are accustomed to filling out your own tax forms, a will calls for experienced legal help. You also need to assign power of attorney to someone who will make decisions for you when you no longer can. Your lawyer will keep the original copy of the will in the firm's safe or in one they have at a bank. Be sure your family knows who has the key.

You're never too young to have a will, which can be kept up-to-date by a codicil. You can send a handwritten letter to the executor of your will to outline your wishes for specific pieces of furniture, jewelry, or art to be given to particular people, rather than being equally divided among family members. My mother had a blank book in which she specified every item. Her thoughtfulness made it easy for me to carry out her wishes. There it was, set down in her own handwriting in her familiar green ink.

Another important record to keep is your financial inventory, listing all your holdings. Recording where you have your money is extremely important because if you don't, your family will be scrambling around, fishing through file folders and desk drawers for any

All that live must die, / Passing through nature to eternity.

WILLIAM SHAKESPEARE

With every friend I love who has been taken into the brown bosom of the earth a part of me has been buried there; but their contribution to my being of happiness, strength and understanding remains to sustain me in an altered world.

HELEN KELLER

clues they can find. Put one trusted family member or friend in charge of knowing exactly where this death document file is so that your wishes will be carried out. If no will is left behind, the state could equally divide your money and holdings among your spouse and children. But many people prefer to leave everything to their spouse.

We all have difficulty with money because it can become an emotionally loaded issue. This is your chance to make it clear where your money is and to whom you want to entrust it when you die. Just as it's not possible to love every person you're related to equally, many people do not distribute their money evenly. Even an ungrateful, unloving child feels he or she has a legal hold over a fair share of the estate's assets. But when the will is read, the parent's wishes for the distribution of the money offer a potent realization. Peter has legal cases where children become so frustrated and angry that they sue the estate.

We can live in peace when we have selected a guardian for our children, when we've allocated our wishes for our business, and when we have a table-of-contents page in our death document file that has the telephone numbers of the lawyer, the financial advisor, the family doctor, the bank, and the person chosen to exercise power of attorney. The financial inventory pages should list all loans, all credit card accounts, all charge accounts at local stores. If there is any cash in a locked box, have the key inside an envelope indicating in a note where the box is or state the code to the combination. Having your affairs up-to-date when you're thriving is a wonderful way to live because it will allow you to let go, in your dying, with grace and order, free from doubt. It's possible for you to be clear and illuminate those you love after you die, distributing your material goods to the proper people and charities.

There is no cure for birth and death save to enjoy the interval.

GEORGE SANTAYANA

Doing these things now and making all the necessary arrangements sets you free. See advisors and friends. Give presents and your presence to others. Take that wonderful trip with your children. The best way to live is to be prepared for your death both physically and spiritually. By keeping your life up-to-date, not perfectly but reasonably well, you lift a burden not only for you but for everyone who loves you.

Plan Your Funeral I love planning my funeral, with one exception: I want to be alive to see and experience it! Not only do I want spring flowers, regardless of the month in which I die, I want a bugle played to bring my essence back to my camp and counselor days, the summers spent on those beautiful lakes in Maine and New Hampshire.

After the church service, I want a celebration. The whole event will be much like a wedding. Tears and laughter. Family, friends, flowers, music, and words about beauty, grace, joy, and love. There will be good friends, good food, good wines, and goodness in the air.

The funeral allows family, friends, and colleagues to adjust to the loss and pay their respects. That's good. Remember, it's a celebration for them. It's a celebration to remember a loved one's life, a time when each of us is able to reflect, conjuring recollections of someone who was and will continue to be meaningful to us. A service or gathering is an opportunity for people whose lives were touched by this person to share their memories, tell stories, and support one another as they deal with this loss. This event has healing power. Here we can say good-bye and let go. My friend John Coburn believes you can learn a great deal at this service about the character of

Do not stand at my grave and weep. / I am not there. I do not sleep. / I am a thousand winds that blow. / I am the diamond glint on snow. / I am the sunlight on ripened grain. / I am the gentle Autumn rain. / When you wake in the morning hush, / I am the swift, uplifting rush / Of quiet birds in circling flight. / I am the soft starlight at night. / Do not stand at my grave and weep. / I am not there. I do not sleep.

INDIAN MEMORIAL,
ANONYMOUS

The hour which gives us
life begins to take it away.

SENECA

the person who died. The virtue of one person can live on because of his or her example, encouragement, and inspiration. Eleanor McMillen Brown is with me every day because her teachings and her example live on in me.

Peter recently gave a eulogy at the memorial service for a friend of forty-seven years. The ceremony was held at his family's home in Paget, Bermuda. The setting of nature, sky, water, and sun provided a beautiful backdrop for his words to family and friends:

John Webber Hornburg loved beauty, loved life, every moment, loved his family—Polly, Suzannah, Lisa, and his constellation of friends, here and abroad.

John felt exhilaration and joy in the snows of Minnesota, of Big Sky, Montana, the azure crystal sea around Bermuda, flowering trees, hibiscus, bougainvillea, poinciana, oleander, the pink sands, and heavenly ocean breezes. "He is a thousand winds that blow," in the ancient Indian poem.

He was a grand, stylish man, a noble man. As Ralph Waldo Emerson would say, his immortality is in the fact we all will *remember* John, remember him and rejoice in his versatile gift of himself to us.

For these reasons, we are here at his and Polly's beloved house, Stanwick, not to mourn and be saddened, for this confounds immortality, but rather to *celebrate* his life.

Three thoughts we can share with John:

One: *Divinity* is within each of us.

Two: *Words of 1 Corinthians 15:51–52:* "...we shall all

be changed, in a moment, in the twinkling of an eye, at the last trumpet. For the trumpet shall sound and the dead shall be raised incorruptible and we shall be changed."

Three: *We are the choir and we sing to John:* "And He will raise you up on eagle's wings, bear you on the breath of dawn, make you shine like the sun, and hold you in his hands."

As the service ended in the garden, the rector announced that four of John's friends would go up the hill in front of the congregation and would, at John's request, fire off four shotguns, north, east, south and west. The shells contained John's cremated ashes, now part of the land, the sky, and the sea. Peter shot to the south.

What will you wish for your final service or gathering? What place will you select? What colors do you want your friends and family to wear? A friend who died while waiting for a heart transplant requested everyone wear pastels. He was buried in a simple pine box covered with his favorite spring flowers.

Who do you want to speak at the service or reception? What will the karma be in the space you plan for this final gathering? Who will be there? Who will laugh? Who will cry? Who will comfort your children and grandchildren?

If you believe the soul mysteriously leaves the body at the time of transition, that the death is of the flesh, not the spirit, then you might question the importance of a burial. I felt cremation seemed appropriate until I went to a friend's wake. As I knelt in front of Kay's coffin surrounded by

We rarely find anyone who can say he has lived a happy life, and who, content with his life, can retire from the world like a satisfied guest.

VIRGIL

the spring flowers I love, knowing they were her favorites, too, I had a meaningful moment when I felt such peace. Kneeling beside her coffin I decided not to be cremated. Now, I think I want to be buried under the colorful lilac tree in our backyard or under the pebbles of our Zen garden. I've already talked with a younger friend who promises me he'll bury me personally if he's alive.

Plans for your funeral or memorial service or gathering should be kept in a file, with all your up-to-date will papers. The more details you specify, the easier it will be on those who have to carry out your wishes while grieving over your loss.

When I was young, I was disturbed that people could eat food, drink, and laugh, carry on, just after someone's funeral. Now I realize that just as we eat the wedding cake, toast the bride and groom with champagne, we continue the life of the person we loved through our love of life and of each other. Death is as natural as birth, only more certain. The more someone loves life, living each moment, appreciating and loving everything that is good and positive and possible, the easier it is to celebrate that person's death. When someone dies, the event may be a part of a divine design. We can, through the death of someone we care about, renew our commitment to life, carry out whatever is possible in our own time and space. We can commit ourselves to be as fully alive right up to our own death as is humanly possible.

The death celebration is extremely important. It permits those who outlive you to gather together to give thanks for your life. It allows for memories, shared happy times together. This final hour, when you are no longer on earth, is a way for those who love you to deal with mortality and say "farewell." Up until this moment, the shock of the death numbs people. The funeral is not a dress rehearsal. It is real. We've always been around, just a telephone call or a letter away. Now there has to be a continuing relationship in spirit. Saying good-bye becomes important.

Neither fire nor wind, birth nor death can erase our good deeds.

THE BUDDHA

Coping with the Dying of a Loved One

What does the death of one's parents, a spouse, a child, a sibling, or other close relatives or friends teach us? I can't imagine anything more painful than losing a child to death. All things obviously don't happen for the best. The death of a child seems unnatural and too great a suffering. Many of my friends have lost a child or a grandchild.

But death can strike anyone at any time: early, in the dark or in the sunshine, in the crest of life or after a full, rich existence. Some die in the most shocking circumstances and painful ways.

When someone close to you dies, you suffer a loss that only time can heal. As hard as it is to believe at the time, we cannot reverse death. We need to dwell on the possibilities we still have as we celebrate that person's life and continue with our own.

One of the saddest experiences for all of us to face is the long, drawn out tragedy of a coma where we can no longer connect to our loved one. Even though Eleanor McMillen Brown was in a coma on her one-hundredth birthday, we all still gathered by her bed and sang "Happy Birthday" before going downstairs and having a champagne celebration. I felt that I was able on several occasions to get through to

Lives of great men all remind us / We can make our lives sublime. / And, departing, leave behind us / Footprints on the sand of time.

HENRY WADSWORTH LONGFELLOW

*All thing change;
nothing perishes.*

OVID

Mrs. Brown through her coma. My mother was also in a coma at the end and there were definitely times when I could sense she was aware of my presence.

On Mrs. Brown's ninety-eighth birthday, while she was in a coma, I talked to her for over an hour, telling her about how the whole world was celebrating her birthday. Then I asked her, "Isn't it amazing so many people are having parties honoring you and your life?" Squinting, she opened her right eye and said loudly, "Sandie, you'll *never* let me forget it." Her eye shut and she remained silent. But whenever I'd rub her forehead or her arm, she'd respond by softening her facial expression or moving in response to being softly tickled.

I talked to Mrs. Brown and to my mother as though they were hearing every word I said. No one ever spoke of Mrs. Brown or my mother's medical condition within earshot. Each conversation was about happy memories, times shared. Often, mother's mouth looked as though she was about to smile when I'd talk about some favorite experiences, some funny adventures. You sense a joining, a peacefulness, and you feel your love is getting through somehow. The communication is physical and spiritual. These connections may be difficult to grasp scientifically or medically, but that doesn't make them any less powerful or real.

*"Guess now who holds
thee?"—"Death" I said.
But there/The silver
answer rang—"Not
Death, but Love."*

ELIZABETH BARRETT
BROWNING

When Peter's son Nathaniel was in a deep coma in Italy after being hit by a car on the highway at Aosta, I was fortunately able to aid in his return to consciousness by the power of stimulation and suggestion. Have you ever told a white lie? I pretended to Nathaniel that I was his mother. In reality, his mother was in an irreversible coma from a cerebral hemorrhage in Connecticut, so I stepped in because I knew he needed maternal love. I kissed Nathaniel, rubbed his arms, tickled him, and aroused life in his body. Human touch is often more stirring than words, especially at critical times. I told Nathaniel that he'd had a terrible, frightening dream but it was now time to wake up. Everything was all right. I asked him to squeeze his fist around my fingers as if he knew I was there, if he heard me. I told him I knew how weak he was but just press, once. And he did. We got his father, nurses, and doctors to gather around his bed and, like an angel, he closed his fingers over mine when a doctor gently requested, "Nathaniel, let your mother know you're back with us."

Now comes the mystery.
HENRY WARD BEECHER'S
LAST WORDS

No one is dead until he stops breathing. Think of a coma as sleep. There are different stages of comas just as there are light and heavy sleep patterns. It's important to be sure you continue to talk to the person, making tender, loving remarks. You never know whether or not you are being heard.

When my mother was near death, on morphine, she told me she was going to a party and I wasn't invited. Death is a door we all enter, a bridge we cross, a boat we sail.

In life we're thrown together, in families, in friendships, through our work and circumstances, where we live and where we study. The death of a family member or loved one brings to light the relationship you shared. We grieve because we care. When someone we love dies, we are acutely aware of how important that person is in our lives. Death is concrete, final, and silent. We can no longer carry on a conversation the way we were able to when our loved one was alive.

A Bird called the Phoenix, one thousand years it lives, and at the end of those thousand years, its nest is engulfed in flames, and consumes it. But the germ of its essence survives and renews itself and lives.
THE BOOK OF GENESIS

Feeling the pain of loss when someone close to us dies is natural, normal, healthy and balanced. We feel sorrow, distress, and perhaps misfortune. It is not up to us to ask why, but to accept death, grieve, and move on. There is no need to feel regret. Death teaches us to do what we can, when we can, and then let go. There are stages in recovery from the death of a loved one. Everyone takes time to adjust to death, and being able to express your sadness and pain is the sign of an emotionally balanced person.

With the death of my younger brother, Richard, I felt he was finally released from insufferable, unrelenting agony. But when my older brother, Powell, had a massive stroke during a triple bypass operation, I felt cheated that we couldn't grow old together, that he wouldn't be able to see his six-month-old granddaughter, Emily, grow up or to attend her high school graduation and wedding. No matter how much sorrow Powell had to face (and he had had his equal share) he'd figured out the art of happiness. He loved every aspect of his life and lived it to the hilt every day. I grieved over Richard's lack of happiness and I felt sad at Powell's joy being snuffed out. My younger brother was severely mentally ill and not able to cope with any kind of relationship, but my brother Powell had always been there for me for fifty-three years.

Often the test of courage is not to die but to live.

VITTORIO ALFIERI

This bond is difficult to give up, but immediately, I realized *I* hadn't died, Powell was dead. *I* still had life. The day after he died, I went to one of his favorite restaurants for brunch. Everyone there was happy, laughing, hugging as they greeted one another. I watched lovers kissing and holding hands. The music was fun, and the atmosphere exuded energy, felicity, and life.

I snapped out of my aching sadness in that place, looking around, wondering where Powell liked to sit, what he enjoyed ordering. The next morning, his three children invited us to their favorite hangout in northern Chicago for breakfast. We sat at John's Place, warmed by a potbellied coal stove, carrying on, telling stories, smiling, holding hands, eating comforting, familiar food, laughing whenever we could, bouncing Emily on our laps, letting her smile pierce through our sadness, and, miraculously, Powell was there. He was there, living through his younger sister, his three children, his granddaughter, his wife. We all felt it. His loving presence, his smile, his humor, his tenderness was lifting us up. As soon as you balance the sadness and loss with the gift of the life of the loved one, with the love you shared, immortality has space to breathe new life into your relationship, which you discover has changed but not ended.

He is immortal, but not because he alone among creatures has an inexhaustible voice, but because he has a soul, a spirit capable of compassion and sacrifice and endurance.

WILLIAM FAULKNER

I needed to cry and hug loved ones. I wanted to tell some poignant stories about my brother. But mostly, I needed to really believe the fact that he was dead. I couldn't deny this as I tried to get my life back to normal. The week between Powell's death and his memorial service, I was kind to myself. The first day back from Chicago, I knew my brain would be too distracted to work. When I impulsively began to try on clothes and pin them for alterations at the dry cleaners, I suddenly caught myself feeling really happy. I got some bounce back. I anticipated future events, spoke with friends on the telephone, did some light housework, even a bit of ironing, and that heaviness eased.

I wrote some notes, sat by a cozy fire, and let life happen. I didn't push myself; I relaxed into a lighter schedule which felt good. Brooke and I met for massages and supper. We bought a sweater for a friend who just had a baby girl. I thought of Emily and bought her a pink-and-white-checked dress. The first night I came back home to the apartment, Peter had several friends over. I joined them and quietly, softly appreciated being able to talk about and think about someone other than Powell. It was a welcome opportunity for equanimity. The fact that no one at our apartment knew my brother or that he had died was a relief. I needed a break from grief, and gradually, all the distress was transformed into loving, warm memories.

Do allow yourself to submit to this sadness. Listen to what your heart dictates. Give yourself all the things you need to help you recover. I spent a whole evening with Brooke poring over photograph albums, enjoying a backward journey through all those years we shared. Grief is as necessary as joy. It comes inconveniently, often catches us unprepared, but we understand that a full, rich life experiences both ends of the spectrum. Between life and death, we will feel many varied emotions depending on circumstances. We will learn from our losses and deepen our love of life and appreciation of those we love while they're alive.

O holy simplicity!
JOHN HUSS'S LAST
WORDS AT THE STAKE

Jacqueline Kennedy Onassis

When Peter and I heard the sad news that Jackie Kennedy Onassis had died, we were in Mougins, France. We learned that there was nothing else the doctors could do for her. One day later she was dead. I couldn't believe it. *Jackie Kennedy Onassis is dead. No, this can't be true,* I thought.

As a well-spent day brings happy sleep, so life well-used brings happy death.

LEONARDO DA VINCI

I was fortunate to know Jackie Onassis personally. I was terribly sad when she died. The only thing that soothed me was to read about her, think about her, to raise her up in my consciousness so I could remember her and reflect. I've learned more about her since she died than when she lived. She set a fine example. This is a woman who made some really tough decisions, who was courageous, noble, and full of grace in her living and dying. She rose above all the publicity, kept quiet, held her head high, and left a lasting, positive effect on the world. Everyone loved Jackie and felt sad when she died. But death does not discriminate.

Jackie Onassis had chosen not to be kept alive by heroic means. She didn't feel sorry for herself because she had cancer. She died with dignity, and the word *grace* was in all the newspaper headlines. Since her death, I've come to appreciate just how noble she was. I respect her ability to have maintained her privacy, for herself and for her children's sake. Jackie always took the high road.

A sonnet is a moment's monument—/ Memorial from the soul's eternity/ To one dead deathless hour.

DANTE GABRIEL
ROSSETTI

I think she will be missed because she lived a big life. If death adds fire to life, thinking about it can be useful. I will live with a quieter sense of appreciation and acceptance as well as courage because of her.

Endings and Beginnings

I will end here as I began. It seems fitting and appropriate to come full circle reflecting on the continuousness of the cycles of life and death. Our greatest gift is the gift of life. And only when we accept our inevitable death can we live this life fully. For this reason, a balanced life is one in which we continue to focus all our energies on deepening and appreciating our life, knowing that death opens up even greater depths of experience in our daily lives.

It is a poor thing for anyone to fear that which is inevitable.

TERTULLIAN

When we're here, we should be *here*. And when we

die, that will be our new world. We can only live, to quote the dying words of Henry David Thoreau (which Peter used as the title for his book of essays), *One World at a Time*. Each death terminates a life we shared with someone, yet on some level the *relationship* is always there. My mother has been dead for fifteen years, but recently, in a dream, we traveled to France together. She was young, vibrant, energetic, and happy, living it up, enjoying herself in ways I never experienced her doing when she was alive. It was a vividly colorful dream full of such detail and flavors. The night my brother Powell died, I dreamed he put his hands on my shoulders. "Sis, are you warm enough?" We were outside, it was cold, and there was snow on the ground. I didn't have boots on. It actually began to snow just after he died.

Life, as we know it here and now on earth as human beings, will always be challenging. We're here to learn necessary lessons, which may not be the ones we select. It is the challenges we *meet* and the losses we *face* that allow us the possibility of joy. We can't have life without death. How tragic never to have lived because of our fear of death. "Wherever your life ends, it is all there," wrote Montaigne. "The advantage of living is not measured by length, but by use; some men have lived long, and lived little; attend to it while you are in it. It lies in your will, not in the number of years, for you to have lived enough."

Remember to attend to life "while you are in it." Let your *will* inspire you to *use* it all, now.

My love of life leads me to believe there are great mysteries no one understands. Death is that final mystery. At the moment, I'm just having so much fun living and enjoying life and being a part of the miracle of life that I'm not so preoccupied with the mystery of death.

*Time flies,
death urges...*

EDWARD YOUNG

*Hold him alone truly
fortunate who has ended
his life in happy well-
being.*

AESCHYLUS

There are so many astonishing things that occur every day, right where we are. These are the feelings we have whenever we connect to our whole self. We experience flickering moments of enlightenment. This wisdom is accumulated gradually, as we learn to teach ourselves how to redirect our energy, tap into our divine spirit, and appreciate the multitude of possibilities within our reach. When we're here, the feeling is like dazzling sunbeams radiating out from our center. We glimpse these little epiphanies which lead in toward our own eternal infinite spirit which is ageless and timeless. Our *ch'i*, or vibrational energy, can't die. We don't know or understand everything. We've all experienced situations that can't be scientifically proven. We will die embracing truth and accepting the mystery.

Of course heaven forbids certain pleasures, but one finds means of compromise.

MOLIÈRE

The body is matter, subject to the changes in nature's cycles, which are impermanent, perishable, and finite. Just as life is real, so too is death. While they may be two sides of the same coin, they are still different sides; like yin and yang, they are polar opposites. When anyone speaks about eternal life, it is not life as we experience it when we are in our bodies. We are being and not being. We are not here but we are here. We are mortal and immortal. *If* we develop ways to connect to our higher self, then we will not fear death. Death will indeed be the perfect transition from body and matter to spirit and essence.

Is there life after death? All I know is there's life before death and that light, radiance, and loving energy will never die. We'll live on "in spirit." Those who outlive us will communicate with us no matter where we are or what evolves from our soul, which I believe is infinite. And when we're able to use our minds, our imaginations, and our inner resources to be more and more useful to others, our lives will remain alive in our successors.

Right here and now, the more we develop our whole self, the more we're able to tap into our universal energy. We are not alone, but connected, in communion, one to another, bound together in love. By raising our consciousness, becoming more mindful, paying attention to our subconsciousness—by silently allowing our awareness to make connections and interconnections, we expand our self. When we are able to continuously enlarge our insights, we can live the mystery magnificently.

Emerson once heard that "whenever the name of man is spoken, the doctrine of immortality is announced.... We know the answer that leaves nothing to ask. We know the Spirit by its victorious tone." Because each one of us will eventually face death, let this reality dictate how we live our lives now. The more vibrantly we live, the less the sting of death. Death makes real living possible.

When you were born, you cried and the world rejoiced. Live your life in such a manner that when you die the world cries and you rejoice.

INDIAN PROVERB

PART THREE

Joy,

Love,

and

Freedom

6

Loving

The affirmation of one's own life,
happiness, growth, freedom, is rooted in
one's capacity to love...in care, respect,
responsibility, and knowledge.

—ERICH FROMM

What Is Love?

Theodor Reik wrote in *Of Love and Lust:*

> Wise men warn us again and again not to expect permanent and serene happiness from love, to remember that it brings misery, makes one dependent on the object, has downs as well as ups, like any human creation. It is not love's fault that we demand too much of it, putting all our eggs into one basket.

Love is quite a wonderful energy. I say *energy* because I think that love is a force rather than a state of being. It's difficult to say exactly what love is, but when we feel it, we are transformed. Perhaps the only thing you can say for certain about love is that it is riddled with paradoxes. You can always feel love's absence but you can't always be sure you will feel its presence—even when it's there. Love takes us out of ourselves, yet there is nothing that requires us to give more of ourselves. Love can be a source of pain, yet nothing can heal us more fully. Love doesn't always last, but it is always in the making. Love is an invisible, spiritual force, yet love shows itself in concrete acts—work is love made tangible. There are many different kinds of love, yet all love comes from the same place. The impulse to love comes from our unconscious, yet without our conscious and deliberate attention, love cannot be sustained.

My oldest friend, Wendy, and I think about each

Life is full of opportunities for learning love. . . The world is not a playground; it is a schoolroom. Life is not a holiday but an education. And the one eternal lesson for all of us is how better we can love.

HENRY DRUMMOND

other every day. "Sandie, I've been thinking of you so much late-ly, I just had to talk with you." The feeling's always mutual. Friendships like ours are sustained by loving thoughts and actions. When someone lets you know she or he is thinking of you, you feel special. When someone expresses loving thoughts, you are touched on a spiri-tual level. By paying attention to these stirrings in our heart, we keep love alive. We do this with our child in big and little acts of caring. Whether we give a bear hug when children come into the kitchen for break-

You are a spiritual being, created in and of love...

ERIC BUTTERWORTH

fast, a telephone call to their apartment, or a Matisse postcard sent with a love note to their dorm at college, we reinforce love through these actions.

When you love, the energy to express those feelings is already there so your actions are different forms of grace. In our mar-riage, I express my love for Peter directly, but equally often, I express it indirectly. I love doing small, kind, caring things for him because it brings us both joy. He appreciates my actions, and I find pleasure in the act itself. Whether I bring him a beau-tiful romantic breakfast tray in bed with *The New York Times* or place a pretty bouquet of daffodils, roses, and tulips on his desk while he's working, he feels uplifted, inspired. The feeling is awesome, a blissful sense of joy I always experience when I do any loving act, regardless of where or when or for whom.

When we exist in this loving consciousness, everything we do is an expression of this grace, this energy. That's why I feel we can love indirectly in so many ways that also boost and support directly communicated love. Folding Peter's pajamas or drawing him a bath, pouring in a favorite French gel to sweeten the water all bring me pleasure. Even when I iron one of his shirts and hang it in his closet I feel a sweet sense of connection, of losing my *self* in favor of gaining his presence in my soul. So, even the little things we do behind the scenes can be love gestures when thought about in this spiritual way. Whenever we do something with no need of reward, we're surprised by the inward gifts we receive as well as the appreciation and affection from others.

I am pleased that you have learned to love a hyacinth, the mere habit of learning to love is the thing.

JANE AUSTEN

No description of love has proven so meaningful to me as M. Scott Peck's definition in his best-selling book *The Road Less Traveled*, where he says that love is "the will to extend one's self for the purpose of nurturing one's own or another's spiritual growth." There's a lot of wisdom packed into that one little summation. What I read in it is that we are truly loving when we help ourselves and others to be all we are meant to be. A loving life is a life where there is a balance between fulfilling our own needs and caring enough about others to help them fulfill theirs. Our love needs all the support it can get. As the Buddha so sagely asked, "Life is so hard, how could we ever withhold our love from someone? "

Just as a parent continues to love and care for a child even after the child has grown up and become more physically and emotionally independent, so must we offer support and encouragement to others even when they cannot respond in kind. Many years ago, I had an older friend who was a senior editor at *Reader's Digest* and through his generosity of spirit gave me courage at a critical period in my life.

One Saturday afternoon, Mr. Bob O'Brien noticed me sitting under the shade of a large elm tree near the tennis courts at a club in Fairfield, Connecticut, where we were both members. I was writing. We often had played mixed doubles together, though during our tennis exchanges, he never inquired what I was scribbling in my notebook. But he observed that I did this often, between tennis matches. Several weeks later at a poolside barbecue supper party, he asked me to dance. "I've watched you write, Sandie. May I ask what you're writing?" Without taking time to think, the words flowed straight from my heart. "A book," I answered.

After the Calypso Kings of Fairfield County took a break singing the classic "Day-O," in a tender gesture, Mr. O'Brien handed me his business card. "If there's ever anything I can do to help you with your writing career and your book, just give me a call, Sandie." And I did. Later, he excerpted the chapter on color from *Style for Living* for the *Digest.*

Bob's greatest quality was his passion for teaching. He loved to guide me, and opened the world of great books to me. It was then that I first began writing every day. I can still see his face light up when he read my first writing efforts, twenty-eight years ago; I had spelled the word *paraphernalia* phonetically. He showed delight in my enthusiasm to learn. Bob gave of himself, and when it was time for me to move on, he said good-bye with grace. That was a gift of love.

Love is not a constant; it is energy, intention, and action. There are days when you love the world, when you embrace it, can smile, make others smile, do your work with ease, and reach out to others. But there are also days when you're not 100 percent. Many people comment about my high level of energy. What does this really mean? I'm blessed with health and am vital and full of beans. But I can have off days, like everyone else, and I do. Maybe I've had a bad night's sleep or I'm affected by a dark, gloomy, gray day or I was dumb enough to fall asleep in front of the television set and the violence and horror affected my subconscious. Maybe I have a headache from drinking a certain kind of wine the night before, or a stomachache from food I ate. Or maybe I wake up grumpy or frustrated and can't figure out why.

A loving heart is the truest wisdom.

CHARLES DICKENS

If you have an argument with a parent, a child, a lover, a friend, or a business coworker and leave the fight unresolved, where you haven't made up, inevitably you feel awful. It's human to have bad days, times when you're only half yourself and the other half is plain *blah*. But no one has to have days when *nothing* feels good. Even if you're angry, a chocolate chip cookie tastes good. We may have a day when we drop things, break things, trip, fall and get a splinter, catch our thumb in a car door, misplace our wallet, and lose an earring. But still, not everything is wrong. Our husband can hug away our frustration, a child can make us smile. If one person has hateful feelings toward you and is out to hurt you, that's just one person out of the many who genuinely love you and want you to be happy.

Cherish that which is within you.

CHUANG-TZU

When all we can do is focus on how awful things are, when we complain that we feel cheated and deprived, we become depressed. I've never had a day when I don't find lots of things to appreciate. There are times when I push love away, instead of extending myself to it, which is what I know I need to do but am not capable of at the time. But this is natural, and always passes. No one can run at full speed all of the time.

If Peter and I are not at our best, our true love for each other is no less. The love is constant. We feel secure in each other and know not to take any negative vibes personally. At these times, we try to give each other space. If one of us needs to be left alone for a while, we understand that this is much better than one of us picking a meaningless argument with the other. If I'm not in the mood to be lovey-dovey with Peter, I don't pretend to be. Instead I might say, "I'm going to my Zen room to do some work." By being by myself, surrounded by my favorite space, I'm able to meditate, reflect, look around, and actually miss Peter and want to be with him. When the spirit moves me,

I'll run down the stairs and join him at the Zen table in our backyard. When you or someone you love is feeling off, even having a real conversation can be difficult. When I admit to Peter that I'm simply not myself, he understands and I do the same for him.

If someone is acting sour, it is difficult to make exciting plans for the future, do something romantic, or even have a meaningful conversation. I can't stand it when Peter fakes affection. While he was in the final stages of writing his last book, he was beyond preoccupied. He was imbalanced, driven by this obsessive urge to get the book done. One evening, we were sitting holding hands and I was telling him about my day. After three or four minutes I realized he hadn't heard one word I had said. Peter writes in his mind before he puts words on paper, and that evening, I felt he was a million miles away with his mental manuscript. At first I was mad. "Why are we together if you're not really here?" He then responded, "I'm sorry. I love you. I'm just so excited about my book. Kiss." What could have developed into a fight ended up as a romantic, understanding moment.

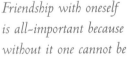

Love challenges us to be constant in our feelings, and we must struggle to stay balanced even though our feelings fluctuate. We ask ourselves, "Does my husband deserve my love even when he fails at times to show me consideration?" Or, "Do I deserve to be loved even when I say something destructive to my husband, child, or friend?" None of us can always be loving; many of us feel conflicting emotions from time to time. You can't be *really* close to someone

Friendship with oneself is all-important because without it one cannot be friends with anyone else in the world.

ELEANOR ROOSEVELT

without surviving an argument, disagreement, or fight. No two people can agree on everything or react to life's ups and downs in the same way. When both people are spiritually authentic, neither person will allow the other to be controlling at the expense of the partner's spirit being crushed. Everyone has a dark side that loved ones need to know. We don't advertise to our mate this weakness, but it pops up every now and again, often unexpectedly. This is the test of unconditional love. I love Peter even when I think his behavior is irrational, revealing his darker qualities, and he loves me despite my shortcomings.

When we truly love someone, we love that person's higher self. Even when I am temporarily off my path, Peter knows my character. My editor, Toni Sciarra, wrote a wonderful book entitled *From This Day Forward: Meditations on the First Years of Marriage*. One of the women she interviewed for the book commented on how two cranky people can reconnect: "One of us has to un-crank." We have to have our higher power guide us to love someone even when that person is unlovable at the time. Maybe a wife becomes jealous when her husband is away on business, and she falsely accuses him of having an affair. This accusation is extremely hurtful and makes him furious. He feels his trust has been betrayed. But, by thrashing it out, not letting his partner get away with falsely accusing him of committing something he wouldn't be caught dead doing, he learns that his wife's former husband had several extramarital affairs and she's petrified it could happen again. Her fear was expressed in an unloving way, but by working through this together, her husband's consciousness was raised, creating in him an understanding about his wife's insecurity. As a result, they grew more loving toward each other.

No matter how stable someone is, she or he has experienced painful situations that are bound to affect personal behavior. Often, someone who loves you will be jealous or worried or possessive and you may find this irritating. But when you look at

You can't sweep people off their feet if you can't be swept off your own.

CLARENCE DAY

the big picture, his behavior could be a result of hidden pain from betrayal in a past relationship. He loves you so much and is afraid of losing you.

We often hurt each other, despite our best intentions, even when we have earned each other's trust. Sometimes we shut down and stop listening to each other, while at other times, we demand too much attention. But we can become aware of the ways that we hurt each other and try to change this destructive tendency. I have found that by acknowledging these failures, love becomes more possible.

I'm not saying this is easy to do; loving is a challenge. Some days we're just not feeling expansive and generous; we get impatient, resentful, and feel bitter about some perceived or real injury. We dig into our bad feelings instead of working our way out and away from them. Sometimes we act mean and our partners feel we don't love them enough; what we're really feeling is our own hurt and pain. When we can say, "I feel bad when...," we can trust in the process of love, instead of expecting love to just happen.

You have to live with yourself at least reasonably well before you are able to live with a mate. There must be a certain self-esteem before you can expect that other people will value you highly.

THEODOR REIK

We can build love even though we may not feel it. Nowhere in our lives is there a greater payoff for the thoughtfulness and care we put into managing love's many fluctuations. To keep love alive, we must always take care to act in each other's best interests. Love is always testing our sense of balance and stability. Love brings conflicting emotions. Love is indeed a challenge, but it is a challenge with immeasurable rewards. Love can make our spirits soar. And, as many wise people before me have said, love generates love.

When I look at Alexandra or Brooke or even think about them, I'm floating on a cloud. When I listen to Peter tell a story to his family or friends or hear him argue in court or when I attend one of his lectures, I'm puffed up with a sweet sense of this good, affectionate energy.

Eknath Easwaran teaches us about the forces that pull us in two directions in *Words to Live By: Inspiration for Every Day:*

> As human beings we have a divided nature—partly physical, but essentially spiritual. We are constantly battered by two conflicting forces. One force is the fierce downward thrust of our past conditioning as separate, self-oriented, physical creatures. Yet built into our very nature is an inner drive that will not let us be satisfied with a life governed only by biological laws. Some inner evolutionary imperative is constantly exhorting us to grow, to reach for the highest we can conceive.

Whoever lives true life will love true love.
ELIZABETH BARRETT BROWNING

"High rests on low," explained Lao-tzu. The mask and what's behind the mask is the same person. Sometimes we may have to express love through our actions.

When the Buddha instructs us, "Do not seek perfection in a changing world. Instead, perfect your love," he is not saying that love is a state of perfection, but rather that we can love better by putting more effort into being loving.

Loving Ourselves First

One day in Sunday school, the minister of a small Congregational church in Putnam, Connecticut, asked the children in his congregation to write down what he or she thought

God wanted from each of them. The class had been taught that "God is love." The minister showed the children a special box into which each was asked to place an answer. As each child lifted the lid of the box, a mirror inside the lid reflected the child. Surprised, each child smiled at his or her own reflection in the glass; the minister's lesson that day was that all love required of the children was that they be themselves.

This simple lesson reveals a profound truth about the source of our love. The place where we begin to create our ability to love is within ourselves. Love requires enormous depth of respect for the integrity and dignity of a human life. Dr. Deepak Chopra offers the following exercise to remind people from where the source of love flows: "Write down this affirmation: I am perfect as I am. Everything in my life is working toward my ultimate goal. I am loved and I am love." He continues, "Love is part of essential human nature. We recognize it because it vibrates in us, however far below the conscious level. Being able to live from this level brings complete fulfillment." Love is only possible when you respect and appreciate yourself for who you really are.

Well, now that we have seen each other, said the Unicorn, if you believe in me, I'll believe in you. Is that a bargain?

LEWIS CARROLL

Love comes to those who love. Therefore, what better place to begin than with yourself? When we love ourselves, we are investing in our greatest resource. Loving ourselves increases our reserves of love. When we know how to love ourselves we automatically know more about what it means to love. Some of us question our ability to love because we see what difficulty we have in loving ourselves; we can learn from this. After all, how can we love another if we cannot love ourselves? How can we know what love is, or what it feels like, if we cannot feel its grace within ourselves? We cannot love another without loving ourselves because, in fact, they are the same thing.

Come out of the circle of time and find yourself in the circle of love.

DEEPAK CHOPRA

If we don't possess qualities in ourselves we *feel* are worth loving, can we truly value another person's love for us? Haven't there been times when your self-love was low and you found it hard to open up to another person's love? Think of all the bitter, unhappy people you know, even those in your family. These lost souls are hollow in their center, sometimes trying to tear down, break down, or drag you down because you have figured out the key to happiness, which is love. What could be a greater threat to a needy, insecure, unloving person than to experience the unfolding and blossoming of a happy person?

Before we can grow to be more honest in love, we have to be sincere and true to ourselves. Loving energy becomes blocked when we conform to the ways of others as a result of our lack of confidence to be able to live in harmony with ourselves. "If a man can truly enjoy his existence," Montaigne wrote, "he is divine." Devoting yourself to all your potential, understanding and accepting both your strengths and your weaknesses, are loving ways to be. Loving yourself is not selfish. There is no shame in it. Self-loathing, on the other hand, is selfish and destructive; it deprives both you and others of your best self, of all your loving energy. "A man cannot get rid of himself in favor of an artificial personality," explained Dr. Carl Jung. Love never requires us to be someone we are not.

The path to our loving energy is navigated through loving ourselves first, and from there, extending ourselves to others. Though it's not easy to achieve this, as I've said, the payoff is extraordinary. I realize how much I've grown in the past thirty-five years. The biggest lesson I've had to learn (and the most painful one) is that no one else's love can ever reach my soul if I don't have my heart open to receive it. When I was young, I was as insecure as most of us were, and I felt others could fill my well for me. I thought that if I was a good person, others would love me and I'd become a happy wife or daughter or mother or friend. The hard part of maturity is how much work you have to do to accept yourself, to appreciate who you are, and to find pleasure in your own company. Slowly, I learned not to put myself down or put myself last, but to be a parallel presence in the life of those I loved the most.

I had to learn how to really love myself after feelings of failure at love because of a divorce. I feel the key is in becoming receptive to love, so it can pour into us, flow through us, and expand us. None of this is possible if we don't love ourselves, because we'll automatically guard ourselves from others if we don't even feel worthy of our own love.

When I was a nationally ranked tennis player, my feet got a lot of action as well as friction. I lived in sneakers. As a result, my feet look like those of a ballerina, outside of the graceful toe shoes. I was petrified to ever let anyone (and I mean anyone) see my ugly feet. At sixteen in Japan, I discovered white "tabi," the white cotton, shoelike sock worn by the Japanese inside wooden clogs. I bought a bunch. Wearing them I felt chic, when everyone else was barefooted. I had Zen style. What a strange, specific barrier between me and freedom, to loathe the appearance of my feet so much that I put effort into disguising them. Rather than realizing how many great movements they'd made, I was self-critical.

When my mother lay in a coma in a hospital in Connecticut, dying of cancer, I had plenty of time to stare at her perfect, gorgeous feet. Sixteen years later, my brother Powell lay motionless in the intensive care ward in a Chicago hospital and, again, there I was, confronted by another pair of perfect, gorgeous, family feet. But despite their aesthetic inferiority, I've

No man is an island entire of itself; every man is a piece of the continent, a part of the main.

JOHN DONNE

learned to love my feet because they're mine. I'm alive, vertical, and they're extremely useful to me. After a bath and some sweet-smelling powder, I often sit in lotus position on an exercise mat, deep in contemplation, sometimes focusing on my feet. *Yes, you wonderful feet. You've been so good to me,* I think. Sometimes I'm even agile enough to stretch down to give them a loving kiss.

Joy and openness come from our own contented heart.

THE BUDDHA

For too many of us, it takes a lifetime to realize these truths; we are slow learners. Perhaps we finally learn to appreciate the value of our love as we get older because as we age, our opportunities become more precious as they diminish. We realize there will be fewer sunsets, fewer endless summers, and fewer mountains to climb. As we grow older, our flaws, setbacks, and tragedies make us capable of greater understanding, kindness, and wisdom; by this point, we realize that each of us alone carries the key that frees the love imprisoned in our hearts.

Letting Go of the Past Frees Up Loving Energy

Loving can be a risk; it often takes courage. Sadly, we often feel we don't have the strength or freedom to find love within ourselves because we are often stuck in neediness, dependency, resentments, or anger. We sometimes imagine others as being deliberately withholding or hurtful to us. Instead of extending ourselves we pull back to protect ourselves from pain. Often, we attribute our hurt feelings to how we were treated in the past. Though we may have good reasons to feel pain about our childhood, dwelling on the pain of the past gives it too much power over our present. When we cannot let go of our childhood pain, our flow of loving energy becomes blocked; we hold on with white knuckles to the pains and disappointments from the past.

Everyone has disappointments from the past, and those of you who were abused have deep-seated pain that is especially difficult to shed. I'm sure you feel cheated out of your childhood and harbor a lot of anger, depending on the degree of your suffering and bitterness. But the only part of our lives we absolutely can't change or improve is our past. If we had a bad time as a child, why extend the pain by dwelling in a dark world and dragging others down a black hole with you? The abuse will only continue to grow and fester as long as you allow it to by not letting go. Until we confront abuse or pain from our past and move on, we will block the enormous transcending loving energy waiting to breathe through us, cleanse us, refresh us, and fill us with grace.

If instead of a gem, or even a flower, we should cast the gift of a loving thought into the heart of a friend; that would be giving as the angels give.

GEORGE MACDONALD

Many of us have difficulty letting go and making the courageous leap to reach for our own potential. When we view ourselves as victims of our childhood, we see ourselves as victims of others as adults, incapable of using our resources. We all have reasons to feel unloving. There is not one of us who hasn't at one time or another been hampered instead of having been helped by our parents' behavior. None of us had a perfect mother or father. Parents often have very particular ideas of who or what their children should grow to become, and they can over-control instead of nurture our potential. I'm not saying that raising children is simple and that parents should always know how to nurture, but when parents disregard their children's own identities they deprive them of a fundamental sense that it is good to be themselves. Often when parents do things for our "own good," our real needs get lost in the translation.

One overly concerned mother felt her five-year-old daughter was plump, so Janet was given skim milk and forbidden to eat any sweets or snacks between meals. Maybe Janet was a bit on the heavy side of the weight spectrum, but she also was one of the sweetest, most adorable little girls I ever knew. By the time she was a teenager, Janet was swamped with insecurities, including the fear of obesity, and had no self-esteem. One morning before breakfast, Janet went out to the garage and poisoned herself with carbon monoxide gas.

As a spiritual being you always have the freedom to love.

ERIC BUTTERWORTH

Lots of girls are a bit chunky or chubby when they're little and they tend to trim down when they discover boys. How could a mother deprive her child of ever knowing the taste of ice cream or chocolate cake without having to sneak the dessert and feel guilty? Eating sweets is part of being young. That's probably the real reason we're given a second set of teeth! When a child grows up feeling she's not accepted as she is, trouble, even tragedy, follows. Janet was adopted, so her childhood plumpness could have been a biological trait.

The way I was introduced to tennis was pretty casual. One August, I came home from camp in Maine and my parents invited me to play tennis with them. I was thrilled. This was a real treat for me because I really didn't know how to play the game. My parents were smart to introduce the sport to me in this fashion. They made sure I fell in love with it before they splurged on any expensive coaches and lessons. In contrast, the piano lessons were forced, and as a result, I immediately tuned out. Mr. Carlton came to the house once a week and all four children had to play. The noise was awful. None of us had any musical talent.

My parents didn't either, which is probably why they were so pushy about our learning to play the piano. Whenever parents push too hard in any direction, a child is bound to react with some degree of rebellion.

Regardless of the circumstances of our upbringing, we must take action to overcome resentment for past injustices. Resolving to do this immediately speeds our emotional growth. We see that our ability to love does not depend on whether others are deserving of our love but rather on our being courageous in putting loving energy into our relationships. Our individual spirit is a response to our circumstances, rather than the result of our victimization by circumstances. Events that happened in the past are impossible to change, and are unnecessary burdens. A newspaper story I read a while ago provides this example: At the height of a terrible drought in southern Africa, an elephant desperately tried to find water in a dried-up dam. Instead of getting relief, the poor elephant ended up hopelessly trapped in the mud. This beautiful, magnificent animal became exhausted trying to pull himself out, only to give out a dying agonized trumpet before his head rolled to the side, and his trunk flopped to the ground. I think there is a metaphor here about how we, in dwelling on the past, get stuck in the mud and eventually kill our life spirit. The past is the mud; there's some water in mud, but it cannot be drunk. There may be some reason to blame our parents and our past for our present behavior, but we cannot gain anything by dwelling on it. We cannot drink from the waters of the past, and we will sink from trying.

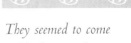

They seemed to come suddenly upon happiness as if they had surprised a butterfly in the winter woods...

EDITH WHARTON

When we excuse our unloving actions, our deceitfulness, our hostility, our withholding of love by blaming our parents and others, we are being untrue to our higher self. We learn to love from our pain as well as from our pleasure. Show me a genuine-ly loving person and more likely than not, this individual has experienced enough pain to have gone through a great deal of sadness, grieving, and disappointment. We learn to accept oth-ers' shortcomings and eventually learn to focus on the positive. I do not believe that any parent is *all* bad. They did the best they knew how to do and are probably the products of a very differ-ent world where parents ruled by authority and children obeyed with no questions asked. The real gift of our experience grow-ing up might be our determination to be better parents to our own children. Sometimes imbalances take a generation or two to straighten out. But it's important to keep in mind that we all do our best with what's possible.

He who would do good to another must do it in minute particulars...

WILLIAM BLAKE

Overcoming pain from the past can release a life-time of love. No matter how deep our emotional pain from childhood, our course must be the same: to find love within ourselves by directing our energies toward emotional and spiritual growth. In matters of love, the buck stops with us.

How then do we turn our gaze from past hurts and focus, instead, on our love for ourselves? We do so by practicing the art of the possible, by letting go of preoc-cupations with whom we think we should be "in order to deserve love" and concentrating instead on who we are. Behaving in loving ways toward ourselves is a good way to start.

Each one of us has specific ways of doing loving things for ourselves that enrich us and bring us back to our center. Every once in a while, we need to take a personal day and spend it focusing on nourishing ourself. Think of this day as one for *your* mental health. There are times to back away from being useful and doing things for others and pay attention to your own rhythms so you can get your *ch'i* back. My friend Sally loves to get her hair cut. This is more than a cosmetic cure for her. There is something about her trip to her hair cutter that she loves and finds therapeutic. What are some things you'd do if you had a gift of a day to redirect the flow of your loving energy?

There is a massage company in New York called Stressless Steps. For one hour your body muscles are worked on by the knowledgeable hands of a real professional. Silently you relax into the table beneath you until you forget every anxiety, every worry; all your guilts and fears float away. You forgive yourself for not being available to everyone. You become aware that you can't ever please everybody or make every-body happy. You are one tired person who needs spir-itual renewal and a break from difficulties. You begin to accept that if someone holds a grudge against you, that's *that* person's problem. Lying there in the dark-ened room, listening to soothing music, being pam-pered physically, you shed control. This letting go of burdens, of trying to correct all the imperfections of others, releases all the blocked love that is there waiting to refocus your attention on all the good in others. It is all here, within your reach, with a little shift in attitude.

Happiness has always seemed like a bluebird, and consists of moments.

LIN YUTANG

Often, we become so discouraged we say, "I quit. I give up." It may be more constructive to say, "I've done all I can." The starting point of renewal is to let go. You know you've tried. You now have to stop feeling guilty and know you are not responsible for anybody's happiness but your own. If everyone understood this, the air would indeed be sweeter, fresher, and lighter. Browsing in a bookstore or library without wearing a watch is a concrete start. You'll open yourself up to books that will affirm your life and this, in the grand design of life, will make the lives of others better.

Begin now, even if you don't feel like it. Offer yourself

encouragement; allow yourself to let go of your mistakes; think of nice things you can do. All of these and more ideas will provide you with the soil in which to grow your love. Focus on what is possible for you to do to cultivate a generous spirit toward yourself, and you will surely learn to love yourself. Ask yourself if what you are doing makes sense for you: Will it lift you up or drag you down? Practicing the art of the possible is in itself an act of loving kindness that will reverberate through all of your loving relationships.

Love for Our Partners

Every love we feel—our love for our partners, our children, our friends, and our community—comes with its own set of complications. But in each case, we find through our caring a special way to sustain the sense of balance and possibility that bring love. When you begin to direct your loving energies away from yourself and toward others, you truly expand your joy and your storehouse of love in life.

Our love for our partners challenges us with conflicting desires for powerful romantic and sexual love, and the desire for stability, constancy, and support. Which of us has not wanted mystery and surprises, and at the same time has wanted our lover to have extrasensory perception, knowing just what's on our mind, why we are upset, and how to please us? Tender loving care, paying attention, listening, and observing all bring two people into harmony. But there will be times when you and your partner are on different wavelengths. You may have a desire for intimacy and you're lying there waiting for a

That best portion of a good man's life, / His little, nameless, unremembered acts / Of kindness and of love.

WILLIAM WORDSWORTH

gentle caress from your partner. Instead, your mate leaps out of bed, bathes, gets dressed, and dashes off to work. With a sense of humor you can accept the reality that occasionally, even your hormones will be out of sync with your partner's.

Love, so that you may actually be what you innately are.

ERIC BUTTERWORTH

In my experience, these opposing forces do not conflict as much as they may seem to. Though the rush of well-being we feel when we are passionately in love is wonderful, romantic love inevitably fades because it is not fed from an ever-replenishing source. Though passionate love breaks down boundaries between people, it does not do so by thoughtful attention, but because of its intensity. These powerful feelings of connection are not really an embrace of the other person; often, these feelings have little to do with the beloved. Rather, what we are feeling is the temporary withdrawal of our boundaries. This cannot support love for long. Passion cools, but when it does, if we are focused on deepening our understanding and support for each other, our passion can turn to compassion, which is a deeper and more resilient love.

I well remember my first feelings of romantic love. That experience took me out of myself like a trip to the stars and placed me in a universe filled with love. I was in high school, and I had what I thought was a date with a boy I regarded as a veritable Greek god. He stirred new feelings in me, feelings I never knew existed. Somehow these powerful new sensations made me feel connected to the whole universe. The world became more beautiful, my senses were always stimulated. I had more energy, more vitality. He was tall, dark, and gorgeous, and every other girl felt the same way about him. When I saw him kissing and hugging another girl the night of what I mistakenly thought was our date, my womanly feelings were hurt for the first time. But I think I learned an important lesson from these first stirrings of passion. I learned that love doesn't just happen, and that ultimately, we are better off when we build our love slowly rather than just fall into it.

Peter and I are a good example of building love slowly. We were friends for twenty years before we decided to join our families. With mature love, there are so many considerations that are of lasting significance. Mutual respect and honoring each other's spirit can help keep love alive over the years. Love based on a long friendship defined by trust and confidence is a love built to last. You continue to nurture your love by caring for the soul of the other person, not by searching for self-fulfillment through that person. Physical compatibility should be the result of this level of loving behavior toward each other. True lovers who want to grow old together will never *feel* old together, because their love never stops growing and merging.

Marriage is not just spiritual communion and passionate embraces; marriage is also three meals a day, sharing the workload and remembering to carry out the trash.

DR. JOYCE BROTHERS

As it turns out, the loss of that jolt of passion—that thrilling trip to the moon that is romantic love—is not as damaging a loss as many of us fear it will be. Though ecstasy may be lost when passion fades, something more essential, more connected to our life force, grows in its place. The Greeks had a special term for this kind of love; they called it *agape.* Agape is love that takes you out of yourself because it is love directed away from yourself toward others. Agape is distinguished from passionate love in that passion is an emotion one feels within oneself; it doesn't require that we reach out but rather that we lose ourselves in the emotion. Agape helps us grow; passion does not—even though it feels so good.

With agape we become a resource to help the lives of others. We're not separated but connected. When my brother Powell's condition turned grave, I was devastated, knowing that I had to accept this huge loss in my life. But being with his wife, Fran, and his children brought me away from my own needs and created a connection that felt universal. Everyone was sad—the doctors, nurses, friends, everyone. By feeling this connection, by caring about how everybody else felt, I was lifted up beyond my own grieving. I transcended my limits of self.

As an interior designer, I've often been called upon to help people when there's been a flood or fire or death in the family. Years ago, a friend called me and told me she wanted her terminally ill husband, Donald, to die at home. Everyone in my firm rallied, and in two days a glassed-in porch became Donald's bedroom. We didn't have any time to waste. We made sure that Donald was able to listen to the symphony of birds in the woods, see all the fall foliage, and have his personal treasures around him the last three days of his life.

Respect. . .is appreciation of the separateness of the other person, of the ways in which he or she is unique.

ANNIE GOTTLIEB

Agape is a love we nurture for our partners, our children, our friends, and our community. Each time we extend ourselves in the interests of the spiritual development of another, our own dissatisfaction and unhappiness are supplanted by feelings of generosity and joy. Giving of ourselves is actually a selfish act because when we set out to help one another, we end up feeling good about ourselves. We are enlarged by our actions. When passion is replaced with a deep and abiding mutual respect for and support of one another's spiritual being, we become whole and truly alive.

Our love for our husbands and wives also involves a struggle for balance and contentment. We have so many misguided expectations about what married love should be: We are responsible for each other's happiness; we must always do what is asked of us; others' needs must never stand in the way of our own—

or always will; we should never be angry; we must be able to be totally dependent on each other and no one else.

When you're courting, you're on a high. You feel the situation is perfect, without any caring or attention on your part. You haven't seen (or you are oblivious to) the irritating habits, the sloppy side of your mate. You're young and say, "I love you" with little thought. You decide you want to spend the rest of your lives together.

The more he gives to others, the more he possesses of his own.

LAO-TZU

You gloss over all the possibilities of what could transpire in a marriage. But in time you begin to become aware of the potential difficulties, medical problems, financial setbacks. You realize that the free time from work you used to spend together, relaxing, having fun just being carefree as a couple, can't be taken for granted anymore. Now, perhaps you have a mother-in-law who pushes herself on you; extended family dinners that require your presence; a transient cousin who comes to live with you for a while.

You also realize that before you're married, you're always with each other because you absolutely want to be together. When you're married, you're a pair whether you like it or not at that moment. Privacy diminishes. You assume that there will still be time to stay close to your own family and friends as before, but suddenly, the family and friends double. You felt your life was full before the marriage, and now you have all *his* family, brothers, sisters, cousins, nieces, nephews, and buddies to integrate into your hectic schedule.

Even if both your parents are on their best behavior, there may be tension that tugs at you when both families expect you to be with them on the same holidays.

During your engagement, you're busy planning this perfect life together, focusing mostly on the twenty-five-minute marriage ceremony and festive champagne reception. What you wear is of the utmost importance. What he wears. Your bridesmaids. His ushers. Money flows into this magic moment. You splurge on a trip to the Caribbean for a romantic honeymoon. You expect the fantasy to last and last. You come home to his ugly bachelor pad, full of his tacky furniture, his browns, oranges, and blacks, his crude decorations. But you envisioned bright-yellow walls, white trim, chintz everywhere, sunshine and flowers. It's raining, your skin's peeling, and a mouse creeps along the floor near the brown-plastic baseboard.

The marriage certificate is a piece of paper, not a magic wand. What you see before a marriage is usually a whole lot rosier than what is reality afterward—unless you have the strength to talk things through and work things out ahead of time. There may not be any money left after the wedding and honeymoon to redecorate; if your new home needs sprucing up, this should always be addressed before you get married. The biggest mistake we usually make is assuming the marriage will be like the wedding and honeymoon.

My friend Valerie had been married eighteen years when her husband, Tom, announced he was leaving her. "I don't love you," he told her. "You don't make me happy." Valerie was stunned and was seized by doubts not only about her husband and about the goodness of life, but about herself. "What did I do wrong?" she asked plaintively. Valerie did nothing wrong, as far as I could tell. Though Tom may have been right about no longer loving her, his belief that it was her responsibility to make him happy was way off the mark. Only *he* could have found ways to make himself happy. One of the greatest mistakes people make in their loving unions is in thinking that each is responsible for the other's happiness.

You are certainly one of the joys of life for all who have ever come within a mile of you.

THOMAS MERTON

When this is our expectation, we are headed for great disappointment and pain. The only person who can make us happy is ourselves. We create love and happiness for ourselves in our actions and in our attitudes. When you expect the impossible, you might miss an opportunity to enjoy what you can have.

We arrive at truth, not by reason only, but also by the heart.

BLAISE PASCAL

Dependence presents another threat to our sense of balance in intimate relationships. Though partners should be able to depend on each other, needing another because you love him is quite different from loving someone because you need him. Total dependency on your partner stifles your autonomy, your need for independence. Needing another too much does not support anyone's spiritual growth. But loving another for who he is and wanting to be near him for that reason is exhilarating. Until we can be independent in this way, we cannot really enjoy our connections to each other. If we see love as a generating of energy toward reaching our potential, then dependency is the opposite of love: It drains us of our potential.

Our neediness also may prevent us from seeing each other as we really are. We may need to see our partner as powerful even though, at times, he or she feels fragile. A husband may feel threatened by his wife's capacity to have a successful career, make a lot of money, and still be a loving wife and mother. A wife may want to be with her husband every free moment but he has no intention of giving up his golf games, his fishing trips, and times alone. A husband may want four children but his wife isn't sure she can handle more than one with her career.

I love the image of a husband and his wife being separate pillars, as Kahlil Gibran described in *The Prophet:*

> And stand together, yet not too near together:
> For the pillars of the temple stand apart,

And the oak tree and the cypress grow
not in each other's shadow.

The gate at our cottage is being crushed by our neighbor's
picket fence, which has been leaning on it for support. Leaning
becomes a burden to the person or object being leaned on.
Needing each other too much can put this kind of destructive
strain on our love.

Our love must encompass the totality of the other person.
You cannot be loving if you are constantly disappointed with
yourself and others. Whether it's the aging of our bodies, the failure of our ambitions, or the anxieties we cannot make go away,
our love must help us help each other to balance these disappointments with all our great potential. Our real self is the
self that love must support. Professor Edward Tayler,
when teaching *King Lear* at Columbia University, offers
this luminous insight: "In order to receive love, you
have to be seen through, and not just seen."

Peter lost his older brother, George, fifteen days
after my older brother, Powell, died. He had a massive
heart attack and died instantly. While Peter was grieving, he was quiet. He sat by a fire and read. He didn't
want to talk. He didn't cry with tears. We all express
our sadness differently. I cried and wanted to talk
with family and friends after Powell died. But regardless of the different ways that people choose to cope
with pain and sorrow, we need to stand by each other
as we work through difficult, tragic times.

*And the true order of
going, or being led by
another, to the things
of love, is to begin from
the beauties of earth
and mount upwards for
the sake of that other
beauty. . .and at last
know what the essence
of beauty is.*

PLATO

There have been times when I've been preoccupied with my
work and haven't been there for others in the way I would have
liked to have been. But people who truly love us understand
these periods, know that they are temporary, and continue to

love us for our real selves, our higher selves. Whatever the situation, whether it is being consumed by work or battling an illness or addiction, the good, loving soul is there inside, and people who love you hold on to that knowledge and vision in their hearts.

Loving partners don't enforce rules and make impossible demands on each other that inhibit the other's life. Everyone must be free to say yes, and be heard and respected when they say no. When Peter and I had a conflict about our schedule several years ago, I realized I'd made a mistake by saying yes to him too far in advance before my fall lecture schedule had been finalized. When Peter complained, "But you promised," I realized I should have said, "I will if I can." Sometimes, though I may have the best intentions, I can't follow through on something I've planned. And though I feel bad about this, I try not to allow myself to be bullied into doing things that aren't right for me. We cannot be on call for each other, night and day; nor would being so unrealistically available be proof of our love and devotion. A loving relationship is a flexible one. Some of the people I love most in my life have not been able to be with me at important moments. We must make allowances for each other in order to grow our love.

No man is wise enough by himself.
TITUS MACCIUS PLAUTUS

Many of us have difficulty saying no to our partners because we think that if we love them, we should want to do everything they ask. That kind of thinking leads us to do too much for others. But doing more than you can is not loving; it is a tyranny. We have energy for those we love, but it is not unlimited. Because I love, it doesn't mean that I can allow myself to be split into twenty-one fragments, like the comet that hit Jupiter. Many busy people proactively plan their schedules, sometimes several months in advance. Peter and I go over our calendars together several times a week, just to be sure we understand each other's commitments, appointments, and intentions.

In my book *Making Choices,* I wrote about the art of *no,* which is a consciousness and awareness that you are a free person. Just because someone wishes you to do something doesn't necessarily mean it is right for you at the time. You're not doing others a favor by letting them be dependent on you. You're actually adding to the problem. And, if you do something extra, out of guilt or embarrassment, someone may see you as someone you are not. Every life has sacrifices. If you want certain things badly enough, you may have to give up other things. No one knows your situation better than you. If you and your husband were planning to have a quiet, early evening together and someone comes to town and invites you to dinner, you don't have to make up a lot of excuses if you don't want to go out. "I'm sorry, but we have another commitment" is sufficient. You are committed to relaxing as a couple, reading, having supper together, and going to bed early, as planned.

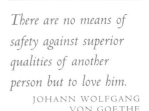

There are no means of safety against superior qualities of another person but to love him.
JOHANN WOLFGANG
VON GOETHE

It's not loving to react to others out of guilt. When we operate from a loving place, we know the difference between doing things because we want to and doing things because we feel we must. Love between us is a celebration of our freedom. I love you because you allow me the freedom to be myself. When one person loves another in an atmosphere of warmth and support, love lifts them both and they feel jointly inspired.

Loving partners try to listen to each other in order to understand their needs. A few years ago, Peter and I were having a party to celebrate my birthday. One of my favorite friends called at the last minute to say he couldn't come. Peter took the call while I was out doing a last-minute errand. Knowing how disap-

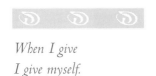

When I give
I give myself.

WALT WHITMAN

pointed I'd be, he came to the door to greet me, kissed me, and told me our friend was ill and couldn't come. As I bathed and dressed I actually smiled through my one salty tear. I realized how grateful I am to be alive, to have such good friends like this wonderful person who adds such richness to my life. But most of all, I was grateful for Peter for the loving kindness he showed in his sensitivity to my feelings.

But people, including your partner, will let you down sometimes. It might not be fair or make you particularly happy, but it's perfectly possible that someone you love will deeply let you down. What would you do if your spouse had an extramarital affair? Or your mother or father? Most of us have suffered the loss of a friend who betrayed us. People get lazy, greedy, stingy, worried about their old age, and become slippery in a business arrangement. Or, you finally come to grips with your inability to be with a family member because the hurt that person has caused you is too deep, and you must decide what to do. Or your spouse could begin drinking too much or is taking bribes or gambling. It is then that you will be challenged most powerfully to sustain your love or to decide this love is no longer viable. If it can be worked out, and your love survives, your relationship will be more real, more solid, and more holy than ever before.

Though love requires will and focus, by taking such action we set off a chain reaction that often leads to love. This resulting love is magical; it seems to come not from us but from our unconscious mind. Sometimes arguments can remind you of how much you care. Couples who never argue are often estranged from each other. I have a friend who is in a nonfunctioning, nonloving marriage that has gone on for more than thirty years. By all appearances, everything is ideal. They rarely fight or argue, but they're also rarely together except when they're with the children or friends. But my friend is numb. She's miserable and drowning in her pain. A good fight might actually be helpful. At least they would be communicating their honest feelings.

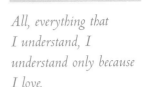

All, everything that I understand, I understand only because I love.

LEO TOLSTOY

I like to get things out in the open. I'm confrontational because I can't stand to let something fester and become blown way out of proportion. Being married to a trial lawyer makes for a tough opponent in the ring, but I hold my own. I actually feel loving feelings a while after we've worked through an argument or disagreement that I might have kept stewing about had I not stuck to my guns. Peter hates to argue with me because he's professionally trained to go for the jugular and win at any cost. He'd like to dismiss me by saying, "You've said that. You're repeating yourself." But I hang in there, because it's not over until it's over, until I get through to him and make my point of view clear. We both must do this before we can return to our loving selves. Love is definitely worth fighting for in most cases. When we care enough to go through the pain together, our consciousness is raised to a higher place, where empathy, grace, and true compassion bind us more closely together.

Indeed, love is a miraculous process; we can build love without feeling love at first. Somewhere in the process of doing, our actions are transformed into feelings. Metaphorically speaking, it is as if we had to walk miles and miles in the hot sun to bring flour and water to someone who was hungry, and, suddenly, a fabulous cake covered with icing and flowers appears as if from nowhere. All serendipity is set into motion by our actions. When we pay attention to others now, powerful feelings of love will come later. It's like getting interest on your bank account; the more you deposit, the greater the compounded value. Investing in our love offers priceless returns.

Loving Our Children

I've told you how when I was a young mother I had certain expectations of what a perfect, loving mother should be, and this would leave me terrified of any hostilities within my family. But when I later realized that I could let go of those ideas and, instead, just stay in a loving place, everything between us became a whole lot easier. I came to see that by insisting that it was my job to make the anger or squabbles go away, I was actually bringing more tension to the situation.

Love is not a higher power which descends upon man nor a duty which is imposed upon him; it is his own power by which he relates himself to the world and makes it truly his.

ERICH FROMM

Our children test the bounds of our love in their own way. Raising children is a balancing act that challenges the best parents. When we add to that the belief that our love for our children must be so steady, so constant, and so unconditional that any feelings of anger or resentment make us question the unconditionality of our love, we are thrown off balance—way off. Unconditional love is love given without expectations. Though it may not be expressed every minute of every day, it's a constant, affirming undercurrent in parents' relationship with their children. Tolerating our own and our children's moods and changing needs not only makes practical sense; it is human and loving. We all can behave mindlessly, blow our fuses, cross lines, make mistakes. The young or old can break a glass because they're not paying attention to what they're doing; the young or old can be stubborn before they learn about compromise; and the young or old can hurt another's feelings by momentary insensitivities. This is life. But by helping one another to see that we are capable of paying attention, being flexible, and having empathy for others, we can learn how to nurture and respect the good in all of us.

Loving parents manage their expectations about exactly who or what they want their children to be. It would be unrealistic to say that parents cannot have expectations for their children. We do, but sometimes our expectations are unrealistic. And though most of us believe that we always support our children's growth, we often do so not in our child's best interests or desires, but rather in our own.

If a father wants his unathletic son to play Little League, pushing the issue can lead to severe humiliation. When a father insists his only child, a daughter, go to Harvard, his alma mater, the results could be disastrous for the child. She may not be motivated to push to get in when what she really wants to do is attend the Rhode Island School of Design. If a parent has a child who is homosexual and refuses to accept it, such behavior alienates the child and is harmful to family relationships. My mother thought I had *no* faith because I questioned some traditional Christian beliefs. When a parent judges a child too severely, the child has the choice to remain silent and guarded or to go away in order to find the freedom necessary to be himself.

To remain healthy you must be able to work and to love.

THEODOR REIK

Loving parents work to help their children unfold their uniqueness from within. When the atmosphere at home is supportive of the child, helping a child learn to trust the truth inside her, she develops an unshakable faith in herself, built by love, that will ground her firmly in the rest of her life. A mother and father who try to listen, who try to nurture and encourage the child's growth, will observe and understand her not only when she is in pain or when she is happy, but also when she is difficult and behaves badly.

How do we walk the line between the power we have over our children and helping them to take over the controls gradually as they mature? How can we balance our hopes and our dreams for our children without taking from them the right to their own destiny? As parents, it is our mandate to help our children this way, without commands or demands. When I think about this issue of letting go of control, I am reminded of how, when the girls were young, we would "de-thug" their rooms, throwing things into brown lawn bags. Out, out, out! I would close the doors to their rooms because I couldn't stand the mess. Maybe I was the only decorator writing a book about children's rooms whose own children's rooms seemed always outrageously messy. I teased them that they were trying to sabotage my career. "Oh, Mom, just keep our doors shut when the clients come. Our rooms are off-limits; they're private." Of course, they were right. So every few months we'd all attack the rooms together. The amount of junk we were able to give to the thrift store or just throw away was astonishing. What well adjusted and industrious child wouldn't have a messy room? This is one example of the fact that perfectionism and parenting don't mix well.

Wherever there is a human being there is a chance for a kindness.

SENECA

Keeping this balance between our own needs and those of our children—whose needs are always evolving—is perhaps the greatest challenge of parenting. When our own expectations become a greater priority than our children's, we lose our balance.

Adolescents need a lot of privacy and can be especially horrible to their parents. As a result, many parents don't *like* their teenage child at certain intervals during this period. That is not to say that they don't *love* them as much as always, because the love is unconditional. As the child tries to break away from us, we are the epitome of an embarrassment to them. We mothers hear cries of "Oh, mother!" often. Doors aren't closed, they're slammed. Jeans aren't allowed near the washing machine.

Everything is the art of the horrible, where extremes are the norm—blue hair, earrings here and there, skewed viewpoints, experimentation in drugs, and sex.

The child needs boundaries as well as space. This may not be a buddy-buddy time, but we parents can still maintain our support by remaining calm, knowing that overreacting will only add heat to the fire. Realistic curfews and communication about our child's plans and safety are essential, but we also have to trust that our child's struggles are a realistic part of growing up and becoming themselves. Being yourself, being available but not smothering the child, are real ways to show your love. When we roll with the punches, knowing that our child is really good inside, we save our strength for the tough stuff all parents pray they never have to face but often do.

Love is fostered by confidence and constancy; he who is able to give much is able also to love much.

SEXTUS PROPERTIUS

We can also lose our balance when we do too much for our children and end up neglecting our own lives. In Erich Fromm's inspiring and eye-opening book *The Art of Loving*, he talks about the kind of maternal love in which the mother instinctively instills in the child a love for life by enjoying her own life. In the Bible, "the promised Land (land is a symbol for mother) is described as 'flowing milk and honey,'" writes Fromm.

> Milk is the symbol of the first aspect of love, that of care and affirmation. Honey symbolizes the sweetness of life, the love for it, and the happiness in being alive. Most mothers are capable of giving "milk" but only a minority of giving "honey" too. In order to be able to give honey, a mother must not only be a "good mother," but a happy person—and this aim is not achieved by many. The effect on the child can hardly be exaggerated. Mother's love for life is as infectious as her anxiety is.

When a mother does not enjoy her own life and is not being loving to herself, she becomes resentful and unhappy, and therefore cannot be available to others. She can be strong and virtuous, but her lack of pleasure in life makes her bitter; she is then without "honey."

Our children have an amazing capacity to give us love and joy. There are an infinite number of wonderful times when our children allow us to sense remarkable feelings of love that we otherwise would not have known; they create a special place for themselves in our hearts. Brooke and Alexandra's support during those days before Powell died amazed me with grace. Their thoughtful gestures and reminders that I am loved gave me enormous strength and peace even at such a sad time.

An infinitude of tenderness is the chief gift and inheritance of all the truly great men.

JOHN RUSKIN

There are times when we can't believe how powerful love can be and then it is proven, again and again. No one else touches me so poignantly as Alexandra and Brooke. Their friendship with each other is one of the great bonuses of being their parent, because I never felt this kind of mutual devotion with my sister. While Peter and I were in Chicago with Powell, Alexandra and Brooke communicated with each other back and forth between their homes in Washington and New York, both sending us faxes and Federal Express packages all the while. I'm always astonished by their unlimited capacity to touch me.

When we are all together, I feel the rewards of parental love. I never felt so supported and loved by Alexandra and Brooke in all my life as I did the week of Powell's death and funeral. This affection and tenderness is so powerful, so real and amazing. I felt lifted up and calm in the midst of tragedy because of the extraordinary beauty of their expressions of love.

So, love assuages pain. When we act out of our intention to

love, nurture, and encourage each other, we stay in balance during the hard patches. We're there, heart and soul. When it comes to being parents, we must give up the notion that we have the capacity to be on call to give our loving presence to everyone at all times. It's impossible, and trying to do so burns us out. When my mother was dying, she came first. Mother was the one I gave most of my energy to because I was aware that she wouldn't live much longer. We must also see that the difficult times are passing stages of development necessary to our children's growth as well as our own. We cannot protect our children from the pains that sometimes accompany growing up, nor can they shield us from the inevitable illnesses and death that occur in older people. A parent's love helps sustain a child through the unavoidable heartaches of growing up—after that first infatuation, self-doubt when they don't get invited to a certain party, hurt when they learn that their "best friends" have been talking about them behind their back. Our child may not want to talk to us about these matters, but we will experience the changes in their behavior. These passages often help us to learn about our own selves as well. In all of these affairs, our love and our belief in our children's right to their own destiny require a certain faith in life and in the process of growing; a realization that in all our journeys there will be failures, setbacks, and problems. There is a degree of faith we must all have when we are parents; faith in what it means to be alive on earth, faith in our own beliefs and in the miracle of our own children's existence. We all make mistakes and we can all be forgiven. When we realize that we all have something to learn, we can help each other change for the better.

We must always say yes to the love of our children, and to channel this intensely dynamic force in positive, constructive

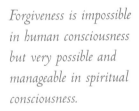

Forgiveness is impossible in human consciousness but very possible and manageable in spiritual consciousness.

ERIC BUTTERWORTH

ways. We can confirm and affirm, encourage and nurture our children to be themselves; to follow their own hearts. When I think back on all the people in my life who affirmed me, who taught me how to live my own life, I realize that it is through their acts of love that I find strength in my own love. Next to a parent's love, the care and support of a teacher can nurture our best selves. One great teacher may point us toward our destiny. My art history teacher, Phyl Gardner, was instrumental in supporting me in my design career. Because she recognized my passion, she committed herself to cultivating my enthusiasm for art history. This small gesture made me realize the power of acts of loving support and encouragement. I was also blessed with an extraordinary aunt, Betty Johns, who took me around the world, opening my eyes both to extreme human suffering and to extraordinary beauty in countries such as India and Burma. My exposure to these exotic places not only broadened my aesthetic awareness, therefore contributing substantially to my career as an interior designer, but perhaps more important, this experience added crucial and lasting depth to my spiritual quest.

Ideally, both members of a couple in love free each other to new and different worlds.

ANNE MORROW
LINDBERGH

Many of the people who served as role models for me were extremely accomplished, happy people. Yet in observing them closely, I have seen that they all have had their own hurdles to overcome. Life challenged them, too, when they were trying to live to their fullest potential. Both my godmother, Mitzi Christian, and my mentor, Eleanor McMillen Brown, had sons who were diagnosed with cancer at a young age. Mrs. Brown's son survived his illness, but Mitzi's son Michael died. By their example, I have learned that we can continue to be loving even when we're experiencing growing pains and seemingly unremitting disappointments. These luminous models and teachers continue to give me strength when I feel weak. Like earth angels, the memory of them boosts me upward to my higher self.

All the older people in my life served as powerful models of love. One of the most wasteful traits of American society today is our neglect of the value of older people. Not only have older people been my tutors about every aspect of life, but they have taught me about loving. Older people understand process. Older people recognize that we never "know it all," that through time and experience we come to feel more comfortable with our human foibles and frailties. Generally, older people seem to have achieved the kind of balance between the desire for perfection and doing what is possible that we are all struggling for. They are more aware of the limited time they have on earth and are better able to focus on what really matters. They drop superficialities and concentrate on what is real, using the wisdom of a lifetime.

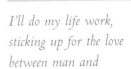

I'll do my life work, sticking up for the love between man and woman.

D. H. LAWRENCE

Think back as far as you can remember to all the people in your life who have taught you about the art of loving. How many names and faces come to mind? What did they teach you about love that you can teach your children?

Loving Family

Author Eknath Easwaran teaches us "Love is a precious skill," and "Love feels no burden." As Peter and I travel around the country, we meet hundreds of wonderful, loving families, but the Collins family stand out in our mind as an extraordinary example of love in action. There's such an atmosphere of warmth in the Collins family. Everyone smiles easily and often.

There is an understanding of the rhythms of doing chores and sharing events in thoughtful, supportive, affectionate ways.

The first time I went to their home in Concord, Massachusetts, it was snowing. As we walked into the house, we were inundated with smells of lemon cake, cinnamon, oranges, apples, and that hearteningly aromatic smell of a crackling wood fire. Connie, the mother, had been in Boston with Peter and me the night before so I knew she couldn't have been the one who prepared tea by the fire. Sally, her fourteen year old daughter, had baked the lemon cake, made the fire, set up tea on the coffee table, and, to make the house welcoming, boiled oranges, apples, and cinnamon on the stove. Sitting there, warming up by the fire after experiencing hugs and kisses, made me so happy. What affection they share. Later, Larry came home with Sally's two brothers, Bob and John, who both wanted to meet Peter and me.

The closeness of the Collins family is an example of how family life can and should be. When we feel connected, when we welcome each other, when we are helpful in our thoughtfulness, when we speak well of our parents, children, and siblings, the strength of the family grows. The memory of this January visit to Concord reminded us of the new movie version of Louisa May Alcott's *Little Women*.

Loving our parents is one of the most complex and richest experiences of our life. It is the source of all our loving feelings. We learn how to love from our relationship with our parents. This bond between parent and child is complex, because it is built on emotional contradictions. From infancy until young adulthood we depend upon our parents for our very survival. Then, in order to survive, we must separate, so we can learn how to

A good marriage is that in which each appoints the other guardian of his solitude.

RAINER MARIA RILKE

Love looks not with the eyes, but with the mind.

WILLIAM SHAKESPEARE

build our own lives. If we do not properly separate, we become powerless in the world. When we develop as we should, we become, in a sense, our own mother and father; we assume the role of self-discipline and self-mastery as we grow less dependent on our parents to guide us through every new step. You can see this push-pull phenomenon in the way a kindergartner cries when his mother walks toward the door to leave the classroom, only to run away from her when she returns to pick him up from school. We want terribly to grow independent and yet we are frightened to leave the comfort and security of all that is familiar to us.

Giving to others selflessly and anonymously, radiating light throughout the world and illuminating your own darkness, your virtue becomes a sanctuary for yourself and all beings.

LAO-TZU

Parents, too, are torn between their love and responsibility for our well-being and their need to see us as strong and self-supporting in the world without losing their connection to us. Many parents can become too dependent on their relationship with their children, involving themselves too much in their children's lives, pressuring them to win awards, to become cheerleaders, quarterbacks, or best in the class; interfering in their marital decisions, child-rearing, and career decisions—or forcing their children into caring for them or worrying about them. Parents can have a difficult time letting go.

If our parents are doing a good enough job of raising us, we gradually learn to feel comfortable with ourselves and our independence, without having to sever contact from them. If, on the other hand, our parents try to control our lives too much, we may have a harder time crossing these life passages. It is difficult to experience your own power when you are still under the sway of a domineering, possessive, or smothering parent. I have seen several of my daughters' friends pressured into the family business when what they really wanted to do when they graduated from college was live abroad for a year or two and teach English or travel. Parents try to convince themselves that they are doing what is right for their children, but parents don't always know what is best.

What wisdom can you find that is greater than kindness?

JEAN-JACQUES ROUSSEAU

Gradually, however, regardless of our parents' hold over us, we must learn how to take control and come to terms with our lives in our own way. You have to believe that you really can follow your dreams even if your parents interpret your actions as defying them. My father disapproved of my decision to attend design school, but I went anyway, not to prove anything to him but to do what I knew was best for me and my future. By loving ourselves enough, we gain authority over our lives.

Because of the many intricate ties within a family, we are always in need of cutting some old ropes and loosening others. The sense of obligation is a strong and stiff rope that can tie a family into knots. Many relationships are overshadowed by expectations, but none is more automatic than the expectation that there are immutable obligations in a family. Here we can make a big mistake. The clearest example of how family obligations can oppress us is most apparent during holidays, when high expectations and pressure to be a happy family are felt by everyone. Holidays can become so oppressive, in fact, that our love suffocates under the weight of ritual, instead of being liberated by spontaneous and deliberate acts of love. Whenever expectations rise too high and become unreasonable, we begin to withdraw our love. Love should not require us to do things that run against the grain, or to give up our sense of choice.

I remember one Christmas when my first husband, Brandon, and I were tortured by family expectations: Which set of parents should we be with on Christmas day? Brandon's parents wanted us to be with them. So did mine. When it comes to spending time with their grandchildren on the holidays, grandparents do not like to draw straws or even compromise. What do we do? I was determined to please both sets of parents for fear of being accused of favoring one over the other. I remember feeling terribly resentful and sad about having to leave our warm, cozy apartment, to get up early in the morning and fight traffic to get to my mother's house in Connecticut. We'd had a good start to the holidays: a dinner party with close friends the night before and a candlelight service of Christmas carols at St. James' Episcopal Church on Madison Avenue. But on Christmas morning, there we were, trapped in our rented car and miserable with three-and-a-half-month-old Brooke, who was carsick, and two-and-a-half-year-old Alexandra, who was inquiring, "Are we there yet?" every five minutes. We spent most of the day driving in a snowstorm to Brandon's parents' home and ended up disappointing everyone anyway when we showed up two hours late. No set of parents seemed to appreciate the enormous effort we had exerted to be there with them on Christmas Day.

Instead of jumping to every holiday like trained seals, our love would be better served by creating real times—times of our own making—together with family. You could design an entirely new holiday for your family, such as a small family reunion centered around a grandparent or child's birthday that does not conflict with any in-law engagements. My family celebrates a "faux Christmas" near the actual holiday

I look upon all men as my compatriots... making less account of the national than of the universal and common bond.

MICHEL DE MONTAIGNE

so that no one is left out of the Christmas festivities. Also, remember that when you get married and have a child or children, you have started a new, third family that is of equal significance to the ones you and your spouse were raised in, meaning you are entitled to celebrate the holidays at *your* home. Why shouldn't they come to you? And maybe bring some covered dishes with them! When your family learns to nurture itself by devising its own rituals, there is room for everyone to breathe and grow. Those days are far more real and loving than anything that is done merely in response to obligations. Love exists in loving acts, not in the obligations of the relationship. Love helps us to be understanding, not more demanding.

To be loved, be lovable.

OVID

We feel our parents' enthusiastic expectations even when we're adults (and have children of our own). A parent's disapproval is a powerful force; for some people, the fear of it lasts a lifetime. We should never set conditions on our love for our children; love must be unconditional even under the most trying circumstances. A friend's only surviving parent, her mother, refused to go to her wedding because it was an interfaith marriage. A recently engaged friend of mine has a future father-in-law who will not recognize the marriage unless a Catholic priest participates in the ceremony. Withdrawing a parent's support is an unloving act. Though we may be disappointed in some of the decisions our children make, their lives are their own and must be respected. I'm not saying we must approve of the choices our children make, but rather that we must respect their choices.

Likewise, your parents must respect yours. You cannot make another person live by your rules, your standards; nor should you want them to. When my former assistant Melissa wed her college sweetheart, she held the nondenominational ceremony on a deserted island off the coast of Maine. Family and friends arrived by boat to attend the outdoor service, where huge stones served as pews and Melissa wore a simple white linen dress and a straw hat and the couple's friends performed all the music for the ceremony. After Melissa and Jimmy exchanged their wedding vows, which they had written, the guests celebrated with a huge barbecue and dancing to the wild music of a country-and-western band. When it was time for their departure, the two sped away literally into the sunset on a colorfully decorated speedboat. The obvious exhilaration of the bride and groom's parents at the wedding added to the loving, exuberant atmosphere. They were so proud that Melissa and Jimmy had the confidence and strength to "do it their way," and they felt honored to be the parents of such bright, creative, compassionate children.

Melissa and Jimmy's parents maintained a healthy attitude toward their children's decision to have a highly unconventional wedding. As a result, they experienced pure joy at witnessing the union of these two young lovers. Each of us must find our way through the world. We are not here to judge, but to love.

Our relationship with our parents changes as they grow older and perhaps grow more dependent on us than ever before. How do we then express our love? Peter phoned his mother six days a week. He would have called her seven days a week but he didn't want Miriam to depend too much on his calls. Of course, that seventh day was the day Peter went to visit his mother, who never lived more than a dozen blocks away in New York.

The idea expressed in the biblical "Love thy neighbor as thyself" implies that respect for one's own integrity and uniqueness, love for and understanding of one's own self, cannot be separated from respect for and love and understanding of another individual. The love for my own self is inseparably connected with the love for any other self.

ERICH FROMM

The life passage I am in now is a very special one with regard to my parents. Both of them have died now, and I am at peace. I have grown to appreciate more and more that they did the best they could, loving me and supporting me in a myriad of ways under the circumstances. Reflecting on these two most significant people in my life, I feel

Love is love's reward.

JOHN DRYDEN

blessed to have been born to such dynamic, intelligent, caring human beings. My mother had leukemia that had been in remission for many years. But just before she was diagnosed with lung cancer, the leukemia recurred. She was now battling two primary cancers. This tragic ending of her life gave me ample opportunity to demonstrate all she'd taught me about love through example when I was growing up.

Love for Community

We can get so caught up in our own lives that sometimes it seems as if the outside world is of little consequence to us. Many of us have a narrow definition of what is or isn't in our self-concern. We may think that people with other lifestyles or of different cultures have no bearing on our lives. Many of us feel resentment toward less fortunate people and think, *If I can take care of myself, why can't they?* By defining our self-interest so narrowly, we neglect the valuable resource of building community. Rather than shutting ourselves down to these lives, we can devote ourselves, in whatever small way, toward helping others. Our community and our world is of powerful importance to our well-being. In truth, all things come back to us when we give to others. The biggest gain you receive from doing for others is that you help to make your community a generous one, and a caring community is a better one to live in both for you and your children. It feels good to help others; there's no other way to get this very special kind of feeling. By activating your moral self on behalf of the community—whether for your

Love is not thinking about it; it is doing it. It is loving.

ERIC BUTTERWORTH

immediate neighbors or for strangers—you release "moral endorphins." Moral endorphins lift us up and take us out of our separateness. We feel good helping others. We find strength and enrichment knowing that we can make a positive difference in another person's life, even in the most simple ways, such as serving a homeless person in a shelter a cup of hot soup or taking a child in a wheelchair to the zoo to see the elephants and giraffes. We feel uplifted knowing that we are more than the limits of our own lives. We feel less lonely in our lives knowing that we belong to a community and to the world.

It's interesting to watch how people behave in a disaster. When an earthquake hit San Francisco several years ago, I was there to give a lecture at an international antiques show. The event was of course canceled, leaving dozens of us with absolutely nothing to do. That evening, the owners of the local antique shops threw an impromptu party for all of us, complete with food and champagne. A situation that invited panic and frustration turned into an opportunity for togetherness and celebration.

After earthquakes, hurricanes, explosions, and even riots, people not only come out to help one another, but they seem united and exhilarated by their actions. When Peter's daughter, Andrée, was a chef at the World Trade Center, terrorists set off a bomb in the building's parking garage. When Andrée recounted the story to us the following day, she spoke with

Love is a phenomenon of abundance; its premise is the strength of the individual who can give... To love another person is only a virtue if it springs from this inner strength.

ERICH FROMM

surprising calm in her voice. When we commented on her unusual peace of mind, she told us of the remarkable atmosphere of cooperation and compassion that had filled the otherwise crowded, dark, smoky rooms as people were being evacuated down the stairs. We have it within us to care. I believe we want very much to care and to take loving action for others.

But we get so used to our immediate concerns that often we cannot see beyond them down another's street.

When Peter and I were mugged one block away from our apartment, the spontaneous support we received from our neighbors and passersby was phenomenal. Not only did a total of thirty-three people come to our rescue, but a whole team of volunteers chased down one of the perpetrators. It's amazing how total strangers would willingly risk their lives to help us, especially today considering the crime and violence in New York City.

No one in our life is redundant. Each person has an important, loving part to play in the world. The woman at the Laundromat, the grocer on the corner, the man at the nursery who helps you select your spring bulbs, the parents of the children your child plays with, the people who work with your husband or wife, the neighbors who cooperate with you to make you and their homes, community, the world you live in a better place for all. We're different from each other, not better or worse. We can love or respect each other, not always in spite of our differences, but quite often because of them.

The supreme happiness of life is the conviction that we are loved; loved for ourselves. . .

VICTOR HUGO

How do we learn how to exercise our moral selves? How do we extend ourselves to others in a loving, generous way? Be creative. By developing our moral imaginations, we can stretch ourselves beyond our immediate community and reach out to deserving strangers. It may take a leap of imagination to think about people of different cultures, races, and religions. We're so used to knowing people who are much like us. How can we break through our isolation and our resistance to people who are different from us? One way we can penetrate cultural borders is by making an effort to get to know people from other races or cultures. By knowing and possibly helping them, we open ourselves to a new world. We fear others when we know little that is real about them except for the generalizations others tend to promote. By knowing people from all over the world, we bypass narrow provincialism. We look at their values. We observe and learn from their family relationships. We're interested to learn about their work, their skills, their talents, and their dreams. When we can imagine ourselves in the consciousness of others from diverse backgrounds, people who often worship differently from the way we do, people with histories different from ours, we can better understand our own lives as well as theirs.

The privilege of being exposed to people from thirty-three different countries at the age of sixteen profoundly broadened my awareness of the vast contributions we can all give to one another if we are open and receptive. Peter and I enjoy attending all different kinds of church services, many of them cross-cultural. Dr. Eric Butterworth, the minister who heads New York's Unity Center of Practical Christianity, speaks to thousands of people every Sunday morning at Lincoln Center, inspiring them to find the influence of truth in their lives. He believes that the principle key to everything in life is truth and love. Dr. Butterworth teaches that all love begins with you.

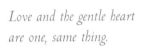

Love and the gentle heart are one, same thing.

DANTE

Exposing ourselves to a wide range of spiritual services take us to places within ourselves where we've never been before. Through this experience we grow in our capacity to give and receive love.

How wonderful it is that each of us can play some role in making the community or world a better place for others. By helping out, we set an example of how good life can be in a great community. Tutoring underprivileged children one hour a week; teaching a writing class to third-graders, donating art sup-

Love consists in this,
that two solitudes protect
and touch and greet
each other.

RAINER MARIA RILKE

plies to an inner-city school's art program; baby-sitting for an overworked mom one night a week, bringing food to a house-bound AIDS patient; reading to terminally ill children in the pediatric ward of a hospital; take your pick. Whatever we choose, we create an environment where the same good things can now be done for us or our children.

Something very special happens to us when we reach out to others: We feel lifted out of ourselves and that's a healthy, life-expanding feeling. Acts of generosity help us stay physically and morally healthy. One of the greatest gifts you can give back to the world is to donate blood to a local hospital. Though there is no obvious personal gain when you give blood, you do experience the joy of doing something that is between you and your higher self. Another thing you can do is make sure your driver's license lists you as an organ donor. Many generous gifts to the community are delivered anonymously so that the donor may experience the private reward of doing something without public recognition. Others may appreciate some outside acknowledgment for their gift. All giving emanates from the self. Because we're all different, we each give of ourselves in distinct ways. Each human soul makes its own unique contribution.

Think about love as a form of universal spirituality: Each one of us loving one another without imposing our own traditions, values, or beliefs, but accepting one another as we've learned to accept ourselves. Isn't this, after all, the best definition of love we know? When you live by this, you'll see that the concept really works. When we act with love as our center, we tend not to judge but to accept one another as we are. We're all connected in love, one to another, and fear is the only thing that could block us from our natural ability to

When love and skill
work together, expect
a masterpiece.

JOHN RUSKIN

reach out to each other in loving ways. I'm not suggesting that this is easy. It's not. *Giving* is the one major message of our lives.

We do, cumulatively, live our loves. I feel deep soul connections to people all over the world. The more people you know and care about, the wider your circle of love becomes. The more involved you become with others, the greater your compassion for others' pain. I feel a shared sense of the pains and sorrows, the struggles and hopes common to all mankind. All mankind suffers. We all love, and grieve our losses. There is a universal connection between us because we all live and we all will die. I can feel the horror of, and try to remain alert to, the wrongs that our unloving acts have wrought upon the disenfranchised of the world. We must work hard to stay connected to the world outside our own door. For there is tremendous love to be shared among us. We can help one another reach beyond the limitations of our own circumstances. When we give to the community, we lift ourselves to our higher altruism. We also see how important our individual contributions are, how relevant our lives are to more than just our families. I know this is difficult to do. As Lao-tzu wisely reminds us, "My words are very easy to know and very easy to practice; but there is no one in the world who is able to know and able to practice them." But we can try as best as we can.

...there is nothing, really, to be afraid of. As we learn this, we grow in faith, we grow in strength, and, most important, we grow in our capacity to love.

ROBERT O'BRIEN

In my experience, love is grounded in our appreciation of life. Part of that gratitude involves having an awareness of our common fate. I think of myself as a lover of peace. Like Montaigne, who chose not to take sides in the virulent class warfare going on in France in the sixteenth century but chose instead to be "a center of love," I would like to know how to love others without finding it necessary to take sides. How can we all learn to be loving, without reservation, without taking sides, in spite of the dangerous obstacles we all face? As the Buddha reveals, "Joy comes not through possessions or ownership but through a wise and loving heart."

At Long Last, Love

Love can be found in more places than you can imagine. I have discovered much about love, but there is much I still need to learn. I will spend the rest of my life trying to grow in a loving consciousness. One of the first books I read at the age of fifteen opened me to insights about myself and my relationship to life and love. That book was *The Art of Loving* by Erich Fromm. I have quoted from it in this book. Books not only teach us about love, they can inspire it. As the German poet Rainer Maria Rilke wrote about the love that can be found in books (his words were addressed to a young poet), "A whole world will envelop you, the happiness, the abundance, the inconceivable vastness of a world. Live for a while in these books, learn from them what you feel is worth learning, but most of all love them. This love will be returned to you a thousand upon thousand times, whatever your life may become."

Come live with me, and be my Love;/ And we will all the pleasures prove.

CHRISTOPHER MARLOWE

Love is synergistic. Love comes to those who love. Once you have committed yourself to doing loving acts for yourself and others, you set off a chain reaction of love. The more you share and spread love, the greater your capacity and your inspiration. I've known some of Alexandra and Brooke's friends all their lives, have traveled with them, and been a surrogate mom to many of them. After my

book *Living a Beautiful Life* was published, there was an outpour-
ing of love from my readers, magnifying my feeling of goodness
and connection. Many of my readers who know me only
through my books, let me know that they feel we are
soul mates, sisters, and best friends. It is in giving
from our heart that we feel joy. You can release love
whenever the spirit moves you. Whenever we receive
pleasure from giving our loving energy to others, we
are able to love ourselves and our lives even more.
This positive energy has the potential to spread light,
joy, and happiness.

Love does not consist in gazing at each other but in looking outward together in the same direction.

ANTOINE DE
SAINT-EXUPERY

    A reasonably happy person, someone who doesn't
have unrealistic expectations of what's possible, who
appreciates the sweetness of life as it unfolds, is, by definition, a
loving person. Dr. Eric Butterworth has influenced my understanding of this. "When we are one with all the love in the universe," assures Dr. Butterworth, "a divine energy flows through
you. Love makes us." He speaks beautifully of our need for an
"inner-centered love."

    I was in a shop in our village recently, when a reader struck
up a conversation with me. She asked me what I was writing.
When I replied "Love," she narrowed her eyes and said, "Don't."
We then both laughed. She smiled and said, "Tell your readers
to get a cat." Then we had a few more laughs and I told her that
love is about loving life. She agreed, and I went off to think
more about loving. Love is available to all of us. You don't have
to be in love with someone, you can love everyone and everything. Love comes from within you; you ignite love in the world.

    Everyone we love sheds lights on us. The more love, the more
light. In Saint Paul's Epistle on love in I Corinthians 13:7, there
is a beautiful part that reads: "Love bears all things, believes all
things, hopes all things, endures all things."

As I've told you, it always important to remember that love is a difficult balance to maintain. Love is filled with paradoxes and contradictions. But when we commit ourselves to stay focused on being a resource to build love, despite these complexities, there is nothing more essential and more enlarging to our spirit.

Do all of us deserve love? Do your husband or your wife, your child, your parents, and your neighbors all deserve love— without exception? If you can find the answer *yes* within yourself, you know something about the workings of the art of the possible. Every one of us deserves love, regardless of who we are or what we've done. Each of us, through grace, is given a chance to live to our fullest potential. This is God's gift. Anything we do to make this divine possibility into a reality is done through acts of love.

Many waters cannot quench love, neither can the floods drown it.

SONG OF SOLOMON

Does this mean we will never waver in our love or our ability to be loving? No, absolutely not. Expecting ourselves to be constant is expecting the impossible; we are not superhuman. And it is when we are acknowledging our human frailties that our love really comes into play. Realizing that we will fail to do and be all that we are meant to be at different points in our lives is an acknowledgment of our common fate as human beings. We know that along with our generosity of spirit, our strength, and our compassion, we will also have times when we're weak, fallible, and sad. This enlarges our sensitivity, empathy, and appreciation for the human condition. When we rise up, against the odds, to act in loving ways in the interest and support of each other's spiritual potential, we can face and do anything.

"To rest at the noon hour and meditate love's ecstasy," Kahlil Gibran reminds us in *The Prophet*. "To return home at eventide with gratitude; and then to sleep with a prayer for the beloved in your heart and a song of praise upon your lips." This is truly a life lived with love.

Imagine the center of your heart being the most loving place in the world. Now visualize holding the key to universal love and unlocking that boundless joy within. The power to open that door and make that connection to all the love out there waiting to be shared is yours.

7

Onward
and
Upward

Your real home is in this place. At this
time. The present is for action, for doing,
for becoming, and for growing.

—DAVID S. VISCOTT

Balancing on the Seesaw of Life

Recall the playground you visited as a child. Remember riding the seesaw? You sat at one end of a long plank balanced on the central fulcrum while a friend (or an adversary) sat on the opposite end. As a child you loved the exhilaration of flying up, and the stomach-dropping sensation of gliding down. One day, when I was seven, I was riding the seesaw with a little boy who thought it funny when he deliberately slipped off his end, sending me crashing to the cement. The fall hurt my tailbone and my spine, as well as my feelings. I cringe when I think of this experience. But perhaps there is a metaphor here. Everything in our lives—our work, our health, and our love—is riding on that seesaw, constantly shifting up and down. You buy a new house and discover an instability in the roof. You work hard to earn your promotion and your company is bought out by another which threatens your job. You bring home a newborn baby as your father grows frail. You're proud to send your children off to college but mourn your new distance from them. The day of your brother's funeral in Chicago, your minister is christening his third daughter Florence. Your spouse gets a big promotion but it means he'll have to work longer hours and will travel a third of the year. Your son gets engaged to a great girl but her parents are difficult. You're glad to have your husband home more so he can help you raise your two children, but it puts a strain on your finances because his salary has been cut. Your sister with whom you are extremely close

Move forward in the flow of life in your humanity and upward at the level of your divinity.

falls in love with an Englishman and moves from California, where you live, to London, causing you to be happy-sad.

Every time something goes up somewhere, something else is coming down. As adults, we may ride this seesaw too high by trying to make our lives reach the heights of perfection, or we may ride too low by giving up on all possibilities for happiness. Either way, our feelings are dependent not on us but on whatever or whoever in our lives is at the other end; without maintaining balance, we cannot rise above our falls. When we live our lives at such extremes, we lose the possibility of living a balanced life; a life ruled not by outside standards but by our internal sense of what is possible and good for us.

One can remain alive... if one is unafraid of change, insatiable in intellectual curiosity, interested in big things, and happy in small ways.

EDITH WHARTON

We regain balance by focusing our energies not on becoming perfect but on transforming each moment of our lives into realistic possibilities. Think of this energy as the light and the love that can surround you.

We can have all the perfect things, put them all together perfectly, and still not be satisfied. This outer- or other-directed road to happiness never leads anywhere but to a dead end. When we're not striving for perfection but thriving in a well-balanced life, we have more perfect moments. When you simply live your life rather than always measure it, you become open and engaged; let these moments in and they will infuse your life with a sense of infinite possibilities for peace, happiness, and joy.

Paradoxically, we may be able to experience perfect moments only when we're not pushing too hard to prove ourselves. Some of my most perfect moments come from something I had nothing to do with, like finding myself walking along Park Avenue at dusk one December day and feeling my spirit renewed as suddenly all the Christmas trees on Park Avenue burst into a magical light. And then there is the wonderful ceremony of the blessing of the fleet, which is held every summer in our fishing village. The boats sail out into the harbor after the bishop blesses each vessel. As the crowd cheers, hundreds of balloons color the sometimes sultry sky—red, blue, green, orange, pink, and black balloons, hundreds and hundreds of them. As I watch them drift away I am filled by a sense of the infinity of life. Mesmerized, I follow the balloons until they are so high above the clouds that my imagination seems to drift off with them. These perfect moments usually come to us when the atmosphere is simplified: you and your love content, enjoying a cozy bowl of soup for supper by a glowing fire; you are in the flow of the moment, together, quiet, loving. Perfect.

Bloom where you're planted.
CHINESE FORTUNE COOKIE

One day last September, I took a break from work in my Zen room and decided to go for my usual walk to the point where I sit on a warm rock, put my feet up, lean back, and watch the sky, the water, and the boats at the end of our street. On leaving the house, as I ran down the front staircase my eye caught sight of a stack of quilts on our hall bench. Without having any conscious awareness of my action, I grabbed a pink-and-blue quilt and hugged it in my arms as I walked toward the beach.

It's not what you have to meet, it's how you meet what you have.
HELEN WORKMAN

As I approached this familiar, beautiful scene, the sun was about to set. The sky became intensely pink, luminous, and bold, pouring its warm glow all over the dappling waves sparkling like diamonds in the brilliant light. I jumped through the gate to the DuBois Beach, threw the quilt on the warm sand, and sat facing this majesty. I was quiet and alone, watching the sunset, listening to the sound of the waves gently lapping onto shore, breathing in and out to the harmony of the ebb and flow, feeling a slight breeze, a hint of fall crispness in the air.

Was it a coincidence that I unconsciously picked a quilt the colors of the sunset and water? Why did I bring a quilt to the point this particular day?

I won't forget the sunset or how I felt sitting on the quilt, leaning forward with my arms supporting my knees, gazing into this huge, hot-pink ball as it appeared to drop into the water. I was there but I was everywhere. I felt whole, one, peaceful, and fulfilled. As the ball disappeared, I saw flashes of green light. Slowly, I put on my sneakers, got up, folded my quilt, and floated home. When I walked up the back stairs to Peter's writing room, he looked up from his desk, smiling, and said, "You look radiant." And of course, he was right. I was inspired. The glow that illuminated my soul was indeed shining forth. Is that a touch of the divinity Jesus spoke of when he said, "Let *your* light shine"?

I've learned to accept these private epiphanies, these moments of meditation and reflection and exercise them everywhere in my life. We can all tap into this core of our being where there is an abundance of beauty, appreciation, and love. We can feel a sense of profound grace in these simple moments.

I am energized by beauty. It excites, pleases, and delights me. The more we care for and love everything around us, the more alive everything becomes, and the more meaning and power things have to delight us.

Enjoying life's possibilities doesn't mean that you and I won't be severely challenged, just as we've been before; but rather that you will experience the possibility of remaining calm even when storms surround you.

When you work toward balance, you will see that there is potential for beauty in every experience of pain. And this can

He is only rich who owns the day. The days are ever divine... They are of the least pretension, and of the greatest capacity, of anything that exists.

EMERSON

I feel again a spark of that ancient flame.

VIRGIL

And when you have reached the mountain top, then you shall begin to climb.

KAHLIL GIBRAN

happen at all levels of life, from the most tragic to the most mundane. Feeling—the whole gamut of it—is good. I recall great feelings of sadness in the days when the just-grown-up Alexandra and Brooke would leave us after a visit home to the cottage. As each left in two different taxis, one going to the Providence airport and the other to the Mystic train station, Peter and I immediately began to water our geraniums and patches of grass. I would be filled with a terrible melancholy, but once I could feel my pain and move on, I would become energized by something in my landscape. I loved (and still do) to take off my shoes and go barefoot in the grass, living the refreshing coolness as I hosed everything in sight. In those moments I would reflect on my life, the weekend with my daughters, the laughter, and our connection to one another. When you aim for balance you take action on behalf of your own growth, and through that gesture your possibilities for joy will expand tremendously. Eknath Easwaran encourages us that "spiritual wisdom is connected with the will." When we concentrate on the abundance of possibilities for inner fulfillment, we will be far more effective human beings. We find solutions to problems, enlarge our compassion, and commit acts of generosity every day.

Perhaps my best years are gone...but I wouldn't want them back. Not with the fire in me now.

SAMUEL BECKETT

A perfect moment springs from our ability to know and understand what really constitutes joy, love, and freedom. Happiness, I think, is an inner experience that we can nurture. Wisdom comes from learning how to simplify our lives so we regain the balance each of us is seeking. We're all boxed in, to varying degrees in our lives, depending on our responsibilities and obligations, but we can learn not to exasperate ourselves with the petty, the nonessential, and the superficial.

Be True to Yourself

Become the person who makes you feel most like yourself. Know what's possible for you and what is not. Know how to do what is right for you: how to make choices, adjustments, shifts, and compromises. Every musician knows that you have to tune your instrument before you can make music. The key to harmony is to learn how to be tuned into yourself.

The windows of my soul I throw / Wide open to the sun.

J. G. WHITTIER

Every day, the way I prepare myself for a day of loving, giving consciousness is to read and write early in the morning. My favorite contemporary artist and friend Roger Mühl prepares himself for his painting by having breakfast with his wife and then going out to his garden in their ancient French village of Mougins in southern Provence. As Roger waters his geraniums and hoses down his stone terrace, absorbing the smells, listening to the birds and bees, watching the butterflies, the mountains, the valley, the olive trees below, an early morning mist rises and the "atmosphere" blue sky penetrates his retina with life, light, and energy. The sun warms his back and he muses about the beauty of nature, his garden, the view, and his work. "Alexandra," he tells me, "I think I'll do a garden theme for my next exhibition in New York."

Wisdom is principally a sense of proportion, more often a sense of our human limitations.

LIN YUTANG

Once inspired by nature, he turns off the hose, takes off his clogs, steps into the cool, shaded house, walks up the stone stairs past the living room, past the bedroom door, up to his studio, his private sanctuary. There— quiet, alone, with a huge arched window facing north, his giant palette to his right, and an easel holding a large canvas covered with quick charcoal strokes suggesting shapes and form—Roger begins to apply the colors he loves and knows so well. With open windows he is not really inside a studio but in the most beautiful garden landscape, perched up high, as if in heaven. And of course, he is.

I feel this way in my Zen room. After reading and doing some writing in bed, an inner surge draws me to my modest, humble writing room, my private haven. Here is where I meditate. I am peaceful, uninterrupted, and fully present. I'm open and receptive and happy because I know how important my solitude, my Zen time, is. When I'm fully enveloped in the moment, awake, aware, and alive, all pressure evaporates, all strain and stress disappear. There's no such thing as worry or hurry or need or greed. Everything, everything, is here, in this quiet place where I live truth and understand beauty, whether I stand at an open window to gaze down at my stone meditation bench in our tiny Zen garden or sit at my eighteenth-century French Provincial writing desk examining a blue pitcher of daffodils, smelling them, trying to figure out how to describe their scent: "A daffodil smells fresh like sitting on a rock in April in the woods after a spring rain."

But my tuning into my spirit, my inner world, doesn't stop when I leave my private sanctuary. I feel sorry for anyone who has ever been in the consciousness of having a bad day. Most of us experience almost a thousand minutes a day when we're awake. Think of all these opportunities to tune into your higher power, your giving nature, your pure self.

When your day starts in the flow of a loving appreciation of yourself, your life, and your human nature and potential being, your day can be a rich, fulfilling one, an unfolding of the art of the possible.

The more you know, the less you need.

BROOKE STODDARD

The highest wisdom has but one science—the science of the whole—the science explaining the whole creation and man's place in it.

LEO TOLSTOY

I take a break from my work and have a romantic lunch with Peter. Our pace is unhurried simply because we are alive and grateful. What's the rush? Why is everyone in such a hurry? Where is everyone going? The meditation continues. Whether I clean the kitchen floor, cut off a few branches of white lilac to perfume the living room, or take more Zen time to read and study, it doesn't matter. I can be ironing, watching the boats come and go from the harbor. I'm not aware of doing a chore. I'm having a beautiful moment, placing freshly ironed linen on an antique French-blue folding clothes rack bought at a local fair. I tune into my higher power by flowing into the moment. When I do this, I let go of everything I'm meant to release myself from, which clears the air and frees my soul.

Today life opened inside me like an egg. . .

ANNE SEXTON

An awareness of ourselves, our strengths, and our weaknesses takes courage; it also makes us feel more fully alive. Simone de Beauvoir captured the essence of this wisdom when she wrote, "It is the knowledge of the genuine conditions of our lives that we must draw our strength to live and our reasons for living." Every artist discovers that one creates out of what one knows; you build your life's work from within yourself. Otherwise, your work becomes hollow. It's not possible to build or create without a foundation. How can you know what we can do unless you know what you cannot or will not do? Knowing your own nature, who you are, what you truly, personally desire, how you want to give back, puts you on the road to the possible.

At no time in the world will a man who is sane, overreach himself, overspend himself, overrate himself.

LAO-TZU

No human being can tell you how to live or how to give. Dr. Butterworth teaches us that the act of giving is related to the creative flow within each individual. He explains that life is a forward, growing, unfolding experience and that giving involves

What I long for I have.

OVID

inner receiving. He assures us that truth is within—not something to search for, but something to awaken to and release.

So when we live, we give—and that is how we receive. When we give of our own self, we aren't taking anything away from anyone else. In *The Art of Loving*, Erich Fromm explains how this works:

> Giving is the highest expression of potency.... This experience of heightened vitality and potency fills me with joy. I experience myself as overflowing, spending, alive, hence as joyous. Giving is more joyous than receiving, not because it is a deprivation, but because in the act of giving lies the expression of my aliveness.

Unfortunately, we often don't respect our nature and resist it instead. You really want to go for a long, exhilarating walk or talk with a friend but instead, you keep working to complete one more project. You cook feast after feast for family and friends when what you'd really love to do is paint or write a little in the evenings. We sometimes set unrealistic deadlines for ourselves, leading us to fight our balanced nature and give way to pressures that make us nervous.

The universe lies before you on the floor, in the air, in the mysterious bodies of your dancers, in your mind. From this voyage no one returns poor or weary.

AGNES DE MILLE

Living in the moment is more complicated when we're stretched thin and often torn apart. One of the worst mistakes I've ever made was assuming I could go to Grandparents' Day at the Spence School to visit our granddaughter Julia a few years ago. Peter and I planned to stay for the morning, then leave to drive to Connecticut College in New London for a three o'clock meeting with the assistant to the president. I'd been traveling a great deal and was behind in all my obligations as a result. I decided to pack everything I could into my schedule, trying to relieve some of the pressure. Not surprisingly, it backfired.

I should have known better. My mother always went to Grandparents' Day to see the girls and stayed the whole day. When Peter and I whispered to Julia that we were leaving, she burst into tears and I couldn't bring myself to leave her. We called Mr. Cory at Connecticut College, and eventually arrived at his office three hours late. This day's experience definitely demonstrated to me how un-Zen and undone I can become when I overextend myself.

We also lose touch with ourselves when we constantly respond to others' expectations of who or what we should be. I have applied the lessons of setting my own limits in modest ways in my daily life, and particularly in my professional life. Years ago, a client called me at the office in New York and became incensed when she was told that I was in Stonington, Connecticut. "What is Alexandra doing in Connecticut on a Thursday morning?" My assistant Lisa replied that I was working on a book and would be glad to talk to clients if anyone wanted to speak with me. "Look," the client hissed, "this is Thursday morning and I'm not going to have a decorator not be available during the week. Have her call me." Click. She rudely hung up on Lisa.

You will do foolish things, but do them with enthusiasm.

COLETTE

There I was in my Zen room, as peaceful as a bird, when I received a phone call from the sobbing Lisa. Sympathetic to her distress, I assured her that I would call the client. "Don't worry. We've done nothing wrong." I called the woman. "What's the problem?" I demanded, gently. "What do you mean? I have no problem," she replied, feigning ignorance. Calmly I said, "That's not what Lisa tells me. I hear you're upset that I'm working in

Connecticut. Where are you?" "You know I'm at home, Alexandra, and you know I live in Connecticut." "Good," I replied. "Then there is no problem. We're both at home in Connecticut. Is there something I can do for you?" And that was the end of it. I try to live on my own terms as much as possible and throw other people's expectations right back at them. You can have balance in your life if you live on your own terms. "To know what you prefer," wrote Robert Louis Stevenson, "instead of humbly saying Amen to what the world tells you you ought to prefer is to have kept your soul alive."

And what *do* you prefer? Suppose you are invited to a friend's wedding that is taking place in Minnesota over Memorial Day weekend, your first long weekend in a very long time and your last for at least five months. Though you love your friend dearly, you simply don't want to spend this precious time with lots of people engaged in wedding festivities, but you feel you have no choice. You also really can't afford the plane ticket and you feel you have nothing appropriate to wear. If you went, at least you'd want to go with your husband, but of course that would double the expenses.

So here has been dawning/Another blue day.

THOMAS CARLYLE

Do you feel an engraved invitation is a summons to go to court? Brides' parents often have huge quantities of wedding invitations sent all over the country knowing many people won't be able to come to the wedding but they'll send a nice present anyway. I'm not being cynical, I'm telling the truth. You'd be amazed at the ratio of invitations sent to acceptances returned.

Weddings are a common example of how we give in to other people's unrealistic expectations of us. We have to remember that when we live by others' standards, we are not living our own lives. Peter used to live in a quaint town in Connecticut which was picturesque, postcard perfect, but everyone who lives there is wealthy. You'd have to be King Midas to be able to buy the real estate there, not to mention pay the outrageous taxes. We were talking about social expectations and customs recently and the subject of Peter's former home came up. "When I paid for our Federal house in 1960, I paid for it with hard-earned money. After living there for a while, I realized lots of people were living on inherited money. Everyone belonged to several clubs, entertained lavishly and often, had tennis courts, swimming pools, and horses. The lifestyle was expensive."

When we fell in love with our eighteenth-century cottage in Stonington, our New York minister inquired, "What are you going to do? Stonington is *very* social." Peter answered, "Do nothing. We're going to be recluses, fix up this dump, and do some writing." And that's exactly what we've done and will continue to do because this is what we "prefer." Amen. We didn't fall in love with our house and escape the noise and pressures of the city to willingly take on other social pressures.

The plainest sign of wisdom is a continual cheerfulness: her state is like that of things in the regions above the moon, always clear and serene.

MICHEL DE MONTAIGNE

I may have been a perfectionist at one time in my life and I may have loved to surround myself with perfectly made meals and a perfectly decorated home, but that did not reflect all of me. There was more to my story, and perfectionist strivings were holding me back. Take my eggplant casserole, for example. I've always loved the presentation of food, so much so that certain things never grace my table. Except for eggplant casserole. I love eggplant. I make a great casserole in the summer using these small organically grown treasures to which I add fresh corn, tomatoes, onions, cheese, and bread crumbs. Eggplants are a thing of beauty when they're raw; they look gorgeous in the garden or even displayed in a bowl in place of flowers. Before I cook them, the purple-and-white eggplants and ripe tomatoes look like a beautiful still life sitting in a large blue-and-white bowl on the old butcher-block table. But when cooked, eggplant turns into something dreadful-looking. My eggplant casserole is absolutely delicious, but my family and friends always pass it up after one look. "No, thank you," they say, and politely turn away. My eggplant casserole addiction has taught me valuable lessons about knowing myself.

Pure reason avoids extremes, and requires one to be wise in moderation.

MOLIÈRE

There's truth here, regardless of the odd shape it takes. I can now enjoy what I love regardless of whether or not it is perfect to anyone but me. When I was younger, I would have been devastated if someone didn't like my cooking. Now it amuses me and I continue to make copious amounts of eggplant casserole—and store some in the freezer to try on guests.

Take Time for Yourself

"Imagination needs noodling," explained the writer Brenda Ueland, "long, inefficient, dawdling, and puttering." I've learned how to take care of my inner needs by spending more time alone, quietly reading and just generally leaving more unscheduled time for myself. I've discovered that if I don't take time for myself, I start to feel empty and imbalanced. I am no longer a whole person. How much time do *you* spend alone a day? How much time do you spend with others? If you're a mother of a baby or small children, you need to learn big and small ways to take time for yourself so that you remain enthusiastic.

Sit in a favorite chair, get comfortable, look around the room and delight in the beauty of your surroundings. If you live in the country, go outside and sit under a tree. Look up at the sky. Keep your camera handy so you can take pictures of your child spontaneously while you're out in the beauty of nature, perhaps observing the architectural details of nearby houses and landscapes. Make yourself a cup of jasmine tea and sit in the living room and flip through a picture book about watercolors, wildlife, gardening, or interior design.

Take a detour when you're doing errands and browse in an attractive store. Don't buy anything. Treat it as a museum of twenty-first-century living and record in your mind what trends you see and what you like. Edit out what you don't like. Don't let a pushy salesperson faze you. "Just looking, thank you." You don't need anything, you're observing. I find a three-minute spin around Henri Bendel's first floor or a stroll through the second-floor gift shop refreshes my spirit. I get exercise speeding up the elegant staircase, and feel happy that I didn't have to pay a penny for the fun.

Even when we are extremely busy, I have my tea ritual in the afternoon so I can meditate, read, or write. I work for myself, but even those of you who have a boss are your own true overseer, because your work is far more than your paycheck; it is your form of giving. You owe it to yourself to treat yourself well. If your office doesn't have a kitchen, take in your own coffeemaker or kettle so you can boil water for tea. Treat yourself to having a fresh flower on your desk at all times. It will remind you of what's really beautiful as well as how precious our time is on earth.

I often work a whole day but actually only write for a few hours. The rest of the time I'm able to fuss around the house, do whatever the spirit moves me to do, but the writing is in my

One cannot collect all the beautiful shells on the beach. One can collect only a few, and they are more beautiful if they are few.

ANNE MORROW LINDBERGH

He who knows others is wise; he who knows himself is enlightened.

LAO-TZU

mind, my heart, and my being. Any creative activity where we must bring something into existence that didn't exist before requires lots of space. I don't deliberately force my imagination but I'm allowing it to speak to me as I'm in this receptive state.

How do you find time for yourself when you're always busy working, cooking, cleaning, caring for others, and catering to their often enormous needs? It's not possible ever to have a peaceful, free moment if we feel we must complete *all* our work before we can relax into soulful free time, to be still or let our imaginations float and fill us with cheer, promise, and lofty ideas. There will always be a great deal to do. I've trained myself to walk away, in some situations, from unfinished business. We have to learn to leave our busy-ness at regular intervals. Many people are so compulsively conscientious that they find it hard to stop until they've completed everything, regardless of circumstances. In order to maintain our essential balance, however, we have to take our Zen time in the midst of our busy-ness and obligations.

When we allow ourselves to exist truly and fully, we sting the world with our vision and challenge it with our own ways of being.

THOMAS MOORE

Years ago, I read an article in *Psychology Today* about obsessive behavior. The article described how people with compulsive habits were advised to train themselves not to finish certain routine tasks that they were used to completing automatically every day. Make half the bed and walk away, the psychologist advised. Clean half the bathroom mirror. Most people couldn't do this. We're all creatures of entrenched habits and have ghosts from the past haunting us.

To the extent that we want to live a beautiful life, we have to become enlightened. There is no way any of us can ever finish *all* our work. There will always be hundreds of hours worth of "shoulds." In our fear of having unstructured time on our hands, we keep adding to our crowded schedules. However, if you set up projects in different rooms so that if you want to work on them you can, just five, important free minutes can uplift your spirits.

I'm an amateur stamp collector. A friend of mine and I collect pretty stamps and I now have them spread all over my large desk in our downstairs study. I'd hate to have a wind blow through that room now! Brooke has turned Alexandra's bedroom into a sewing room where she goes to make things with beautiful colorful fabrics. Set up a gift-giving place where you get lost in the joy of wrapping pretty things. Hand-paint the paper. Cover an ugly slide carousel box with a pink-rose chintz fabric.

I do not think that I will ever reach a stage when I will say, "This is what I believe. Finished." What I believe is alive . . . and open to growth.

MADELEINE L'ENGLE

Anything we do that is its own reward, that brings us pleasure, that soothes our jangled nerves, that we wish and choose to do will fill our own well and replenish our inner resources. We can experience illumination by learning to let go of our clenched fist, easing up, cutting back on things ultimately unimportant, having fun, discovering more about our potential and what speaks to us from our hearts. Artists instinctively understand this; that's why they are so disciplined about going into their studios regularly. As artists spend countless hours alone in their studio working, I think there is something we can learn from their solitude. Time alone gives us time to ourselves to regroup, renew, refresh, whether it's painting, writing in a diary, listening to a piece of music, or writing a letter to a friend; these are inward actions and they serve to reconnect us to our life force.

Take Action

Don't wait around for the possible to come to you, create your own possibilities. In her autobiographical book *A Backward Glance*, Edith Wharton spoke of waiting and waiting in the upstairs room for the footsteps of the man she loved, yet there were no footsteps and no man ever came.

Whenever we commit ourselves to something, no matter what it is, it will express us. Whatever project we start, all our energy is directed and focused toward that aim and we merge with what we are doing. We flow. Whenever we are in the flow of some genuine work, our actions are fueled and fed with energy as well as inspiration. Dancers understand this momentum. "There is a vitality, a life force, an energy, a quickening that is translated through you into action," wrote Martha Graham, the great choreographer and teacher of modern dance, "and because there is only one of you in all time, this expression is unique. And if you block it, it will never exist through any other medium and will be lost."

To keep our faces toward change and behave like free spirits in the presence of fate is strength undefeatable.

HELEN KELLER

Don't wait for things to happen; make them happen yourself. Don't wait for a friend to invite you to spend an afternoon together; invite her first. Don't wait for your husband to buy you a gift; buy him that sweater you know he'd love. Don't wait for your community to ask you for help; volunteer. Don't wait for someone to tell you you'd be a good writer; start a journal. No one ever told me to write anything because no one thought that I had any ability. I began writing under that elm tree in Connecticut because I had the urge. I felt something stirring inside me. I've never waited for a publisher to come to me. I write a book because I want to. I wrote *Gift of a Letter* by accident.

I was at a beach writing my friend John Coburn a letter on my best turquoise stationary. Clipboard on lap, pen in hand, feet in the water, I began, "Dear John..." Only when I ran out of paper did I realize my passion for letter writing. So I wrote a book!

You have infinite possibilities in your life, but they will be realized only when you take action. Begin regardless of whether or not your acts will lead to tangible results. Simply setting the wheels in motion can take you to unimaginable places. We will never finish everything we begin; no one ever does. But it's not necessary to finish everything; the world is still in creation, so why can't we be? My mother and my godmother, Mitzi Christian, collaborated back in the 1940s on a decorating book which was never published. But because of their interest in the decorative arts, they were able to enthusiastically support and encourage my decision to begin a career in design. Everything you do sends ripples out into the world, drawing people and life to this energy. If you plant a tree, you may never see it reach its full maturity; but the tree will be there in the world, reflecting your love and respect for life.

Believing is seeing.
PETER MEGARGEE
BROWN

What we feel, think, and do this moment influences both our present and the future in ways we may never know. Begin. Start right where you are. Consider your possibilities and find inspiration within yourself to add more meaning and zest to your life. Perhaps your loving actions will be passed on to a child, grandchild, or young friend.

Open your mind and heart to realize life's possibilities. This is the best guarantee that you will ever have to live a rich and meaningful life and it will ensure your immortality. If you never respond to your intuition and make loving gestures, you may never feel love. Fill your life with moments of pleasure and reaching out to others and you will feel genuine happiness.

When you promote your health and well-being, you will be well, "and all will be well." You will be challenged as we all are, but what really counts is being headed toward a higher, more loving place. "It is enough if you work," Emerson wrote, "in the right direction."

Learn from and Embrace Change

"True life is lived when tiny changes occur," wrote Leo Tolstoy. I am still learning the depths of this truth. We think that we are living to our fullest when everything is in place, but, in fact, it is in our navigation of the passage between when things end and when new things begin that we truly appreciate the power of our life force. Everything is always changing. Every moment something is born while something else dies. Things will change for the better when you accept that transformation is the natural evolution of life's cycles. By embracing this truth in all its manifestations we gain wisdom to live.

I am not afraid of storms for I am learning how to sail my ship.

LOUISA MAY ALCOTT

Life is a dynamic process of flux. Change is inevitable. "All things are like a river," the Buddha reminds us. "We never enter the same river twice."

Many of us resist change: We don't want to give up our big house for a smaller apartment when our paychecks are cut back; we feel torn when our children leave us and go off to college; we're afraid to leave a job we've had for fifteen years even though we're unhappy there; we've been in a relationship for two years that has gone sour but we're afraid to end it; we fear the unknown of moving on. I panicked when five different doctors all confirmed that I should never play tennis again. I now

channel my energies into my writing, no longer my
topspin crosscourt backhand. We resist facing the
dark days of winter, but then it snows and we're like a
child again. And in our hearts we know the crocuses
will soon burst through the snow and announce the
arrival of spring.

*To improve the golden
moment of opportunity
and catch the good that
is within our reach is
the great art of life.*

SAMUEL JOHNSON

We must balance our attachment to the things we
love with the ability to let go. We know that many
essential things will change: We will grow old, we will
lose friends and family, and we may face opposition. But regardless of whether the change is, on the surface, good or bad,
accepting it will surely help us grow spiritually—and that is
always a plus.

When the truth requires change, even when it is painful, balanced acceptance gives us the power to turn our situation into
something better, richer. I was frightened to quit a design firm
even though I'd been there over fourteen years and it
was clearly time to move on. But I started my own
firm, eighteen and a half years ago, and I couldn't love
my work more. I didn't want to give up my fancy New
York office because it was so attractive, but it was too
expensive and I was spending whatever time I could in
Stonington, anyway. I did finally give it up and now
do most of my work in our living room, which is not
only prettier, but more convenient, too. And the price
is right! My experience encourages me to believe that

*He will through life be
master of himself and a
happy man who from
day to day can have said
"I have lived."*

HORACE

if we accept change, we can continue to deepen ourselves, to
unfold, to discover fresh curiosities, to appreciate all the opportunities, and to accept our limitations, our necessary compromises, and even accept our mortality. Think about a river. See
how it flows with tributaries running off. Water must have this
freedom to go its course. When it doesn't, it overflows and

Nothing endures but change.

HERACLITUS

erodes the land. Water is always moving, or it stagnates. We need the same freedom to flow, to let go, to move and refresh ourselves.

My mother loved cars. I'd never owned a car, probably because I lived in a city and had no place to drive to, and also because they really didn't interest me that much. After Mother died, I bought a car. For three or four years I kept it in a garage across Park Avenue, rarely using it but relishing the knowledge that it was there to help us to escape from the city whenever we needed to get away. Even though the car was collecting dust more than being driven, I was reluctant to sell that possession. *I* was possessed by this car, this underused monument that was costing money every month.

The day we gave the car up, I was sad. Peter had to hold my hand and brush away my tears. We all become attached to our material things. But, by thinking things through, I determined it was time to escape city life part of each week. So, letting go of the car triggered us to house hunt. After more than six years, we have yet to buy a car to go with the house. I now realize that all the time I owned a car, what I really wanted was a house away from the city.

How you live is what counts. Listen to the song of life.

KATHARINE HEPBURN

We can move toward our goals to do our best, understanding that we are not in complete control of what happens. When we allow ourselves to flow with the ever-changing current of life, we will be carried through a wonderful adventure where all things are possible if we understand the art of living. The secret of true happiness lies in wanting what you already have.

A Life Devoted to Balance and Joy Is Possible for All

Last year, the design firm Mrs. Brown founded in 1924 celebrated its seventieth anniversary. Everyone alive who had ever worked as a designer was invited, as were many clients. We all were warmly greeted. Each of the designers received a white rose which we proudly wore on our lapels. Moving into the next room for a glass of champagne, we were startled to see a wall of photographs of all the designers who had worked for the firm since its founding seventy years earlier. On the console table was a favorite picture of the founder, Eleanor McMillen Brown, wearing a black-and-white hat, looking, at age ninety, like a woman with a significant universal message.

Still round the corner
there may wait,
A new road,
or a secret gate.

J.R.R. TOLKIEN

Erich Fromm knew a great deal when he said of life, "I shall become a master in this art only after a great deal of practice." Eleanor Brown practiced for close to a century. Looking up at that wall with photographs of all the designers who worked for this groundbreaking firm made me feel both proud and humble to have played some part in this great enterprise. I could feel a sense of the impact that this collection of talent and creativity has had on the design world. I was proud to see my face among such inspiring legends and teachers.

I never knew that reflecting on that period of time together, when we all worked so creatively, could bring me such joy. Standing in that room, crowded with people, I felt an appreciation for the knowledge that the art of living is available to all of us. When we come to understand that when our best is linked together with everyone else's efforts, collectively, our work is not only acceptable, but can be extraordinary. We all were able to achieve a degree of excellence by staying balanced on our own individual paths.

At the end of the evening, I quietly toasted Mrs. Brown and took a private moment to honor her.

Life can and should get better as we learn to seek the truth, to look for good and beauty, to flow into change, to channel our energies in positive directions, and to stay balanced. This is a sure way to experience joy, love, and freedom. Perfectionism offers the opposite: frustration, resentment, joylessness, illness, and pain. Having learned these lessons myself, I wouldn't consider trading places with anyone on earth right now. "What lies behind us and lies before us are tiny matters," Emerson wrote, "compared to what lies within us." We are all capable of so much; life is rich with possibilities if we stay focused on our own potential. Mentally go to the end of your life's path. Visualize what footprints you would like to leave behind, forever. In *The Prophet* Kahlil Gibran encourages us to "Trust the dreams, for in them is hidden the gate to eternity." What will be your personal legacy? Looking back on her amazing career, choreographer Agnes de Mille cautions us, "No trumpets sound when the important decisions of our life are made. Destiny is made known silently."

Dwell in this place of self-awareness where your way will be lit by a luminous inner energy. You won't always see everything clearly, but once you have made a commitment to respect your true self, the light of your soul will never fade.

The art of the possible is a way of developing specific life skills that will empower you to work directly to improve your sense of wholeness, balance, and well-being. Knowing and doing

> *Happiness (joy)...*
> *is proof of partial or*
> *total success in "the art*
> *of living." Happiness*
> *is man's greatest*
> *achievement; it is the*
> *response of his total*
> *personality to productive*
> *orientation toward*
> *himself and the world*
> *outside.*
>
> ERICH FROMM

what is possible can turn living into an art. You don't need to go anywhere to be on this path. A policeman from Brooklyn has been corresponding with me since 1990 when he read *Gift of a Letter*. In a recent letter Ralph closed by saying, "Hum a tune or two while you sit or walk in the breeze, and if you hear an echo, you'll know it'll be from me." Thank you, Ralph!

There we are. Until we meet again, may the sun be on your back. Let all our dreams and goals be realistic and attainable. The path we know will be serpentine and up and down, but filled as well with hidden beauty and fascinating wonders that will continue to awaken us, enlighten us, and expand our vision of all that is true, good, and possible.

It is the best sign of a great nature, that it opens a foreground, and, like the breath of morning landscapes, invites us onward.

EMERSON

Balance, the ultimate integration of our lives, is the key to joy, love, and freedom. Hey, hey! As Emily Dickinson said, "I dwell in possibilities." Together, we are on our way. Doing, becoming, and growing.

Acknowledgments
with Appreciation

Carl Brandt

As my friend and literary agent of more than thirty years, you are the one person on earth who really knows how far my writing has come. You listen well, understanding where my heart is and what's right for me as an author. Thank you for the pure joy of writing this book, my favorite. "This is the way it should be."

Because of you, Carl, I am a writer. Our friendship continues to bring continuity to my life as well as a great deal of happiness. Love, Sandie.

Toni Sciarra

This is the first book we've worked on together. What fun you are as well as brilliant. Your organization of the book, your suggestions and changes are superb. I'm looking forward to a continuing editor-author bond that will flourish through the years.

Ellen Edwards

All your advice is wise and wonderful. You are a believer in the message and help me to share it with the reader. You are a smart, sensitive, wonderful editor and I am fortunate.

Marysarah Quinn

Babe, this is the tenth book we've worked on together. You are an angel. Your talent is sublime and your sweetness spreads joy. You always inspire my best.

Elisabeth Carey Lewis

You help keep me on my path every day. Working with you is a joy. What enormous satisfactions we feel as a result of your dedication, devotion, and love.

Jenni Fair

You came to the cottage for tea with the girls, you came back for more tea and discussion and chose to jump on board, *definitely* proving every day the art of the possible.

Julie Glen

Your arrival to take the baton, help Jenni, and your commitment to work full time for me is a constant blessing and a joy. Our thoughtful conversations always stretch me and I appreciate *all* your contributions.

Peter Megargee Brown

Our enthusiastic partnership, your encouragement, your continuous love and support, our talks, our writers' workshops wherever we are, the freedom you create for me to work, sweeten life with grace. I love you.

Alexandra Brandon Stoddard

The day I was struggling to bring *The Art of the Possible* into a sharp focus, you came up with the wise subtitle, understanding perfectionism is an imbalance. Our conversations always illuminate whatever is on my mind. I love you.

Brooke Stoddard

Your enthusiasm, sharing of ideas, and talent continue to bring me great joy. I love you.

My Readers

You are the best! Thank you for your letters, notes, tapes, pictures, little gifts when we meet. I'm trying to keep up with your generosity, not perfectly, however. From meeting so many of you as Peter and I tour the country, you've encouraged me to believe this is the book we need, to bring more balance into our hectic lives. Thank you for also letting me know we're friends, connected through the soul. I wish you joy, love, and freedom. Onward and upward!

Permissions Credits

Note: Every effort has been made to locate and credit the copyright owners of material quoted in this book. If any sources have not been credited, please notify the Publisher and every effort will be made to correct this in future printings.

page 68 *A Circle of Quiet.* Copyright © 1972 by Madeleine L'Engle Franklin.

page 176 *Words to Live By* by Eknath Easwaran. Copyright © 1990, Nilgiri Press.

page 201 *The Art of Loving* by Erich Fromm. Copyright © 1956 by Erich Fromm. Copyright renewed © 1984 by Annie Fromm.